"HOPELESS" CASES

DENNIS, long-haired, filthy, powerfully
muscled, consumed by murderous rages . . .

ELIZABETH, with the dainty manners of a
child, the seductive charms of a woman,
the destructive powers of a she-devil . . .

SHIRLEY, so black, so beautiful, so
brilliant, and so terribly sick . . .

MICHAEL, a human vegetable after years of
hospitalization, living from nightmare to nightmare, from pill to pill . . .

They were some of the dangerous "infants"
whom Moe and Jacqui Schiff took into
their home and hearts to raise beside
their natural children. They were some
of the individual stories of hope and
horror, near-incredible patience and
inspiring courage, that form one of the
most enthralling experiences in living
and loving that has ever been set down
between the covers of a book.

ALL MY CHILDREN

ALL MY CHILDREN

by JACQUI LEE SCHIFF

with BETH DAY

PYRAMID BOOKS • **NEW YORK**

ALL MY CHILDREN

A PYRAMID BOOK

Published by arrangement with M. Evans and Company, Inc.

Pyramid edition published March 1972
  Second printing, May 1973

Library of Congress Catalog Card Number: 78-126389

ISBN 0-515-02646-8

Printed in the United States of America

Pyramid Books are published by Pyramid Communications, Inc. Its trademarks, consisting of the word "Pyramid" and the portrayal of a pyramid, are registered in the United States Patent Office.

Pyramid Communications, Inc., 919 Third Avenue, New York, N.Y. 10022

Chapter One

IT IS FOUR A.M. I'm still excited about our daughter Elizabeth's wedding yesterday and I don't think I'll be able to sleep. Elizabeth is not yet completely well, but she is happy and confident. As I watched her radiant face I thought of her as she was two short years ago, curled up into a ball in the corner of the TV room, her long curtain of brown hair hanging forward, entirely obscuring her face. She told me she was being a stone. When I reached out, insisting that she recognize my presence, she sprang at me. Most schizophrenics send out signals before they become violent. But not Elizabeth. Her anger burst like a spring storm, without warning. Homicidal. Poor prognosis. . . .

We took her into our home, Moe and I, just as we have taken other sick children, because we believe that is how they can get well. Both of us are psychiatric social workers, and after working with schizophrenics as outpatients or in hospitals for several years, we decided that if we were to cure them we must be involved with them twenty-four hours a day.

Our method of re-parenting children, giving them a second chance to grow up, is considered radical by some of our colleagues. What is really radical about it, I suppose, is that we make a total commitment to the children. When they come into our house they cease to be patients. They are as loved and cherished as our three natural sons. We experience perhaps even more joy and pride in their achievements than other proud parents because we know how much further these children have had to come.

If you walk into our big living room in the late afternoon or early evening when most of the children are at home, it might, at a quick glance, seem like many another comfortable, middle-class home—except that the family is larger. At the moment we have twenty children. There are no locks on the doors, no white-coated attendants. We are a family. A carefully structured family. And if you look and listen for a few minutes, the structure becomes apparent.

If a child misbehaves, he is never banished to his room or in any way isolated, since isolation is the very last thing a withdrawn schizophrenic needs. He may be spanked or made to stand in a corner in the living room where we all sit. The heavy wooden restraining chair we constructed with auto safety belts is not used for punishment, but to enable us to control episodes of pathological violence without separating the upset youngster from the activities of family life.

There is laughter in our house. But there are no private jokes among the children or the parents. And before Moe and I even say something teasing, we identify it as teasing. For we have learned that our children incorporate every word we utter in a concrete, literal way. Everything we say or do has an exaggerated importance to them because they depend on us to teach the things that will create in them a healthy, functional attitude toward life—things they missed in their first childhood.

Most of our children come to us diagnosed as schizophrenic. They are withdrawn, out of contact with their own feelings and with the world around them. Sometimes it takes a long time for us to make contact with one of them. It was eighteen months, for instance, before Michael would really relate to any of us. But then, Michael had been in a hospital for nearly ten years. And hospitals have little to offer the schizophrenic beyond tranquilizing drugs, or a locked back ward if he seems dangerous.

Some of our children *are* dangerous. Even though a child is struggling desperately to control psychotic anger, we urge him to confront sick feelings that are relics of a sick infancy and childhood, trusting us to take care of him. In this way his problems are identified. It is the first step toward resolving them. Learning that problems can be resolved is an important part of getting well.

Since the infant anger is often directed at me, as mother, I always try to have someone who could protect me nearby. Occasionally, however, the anger catches me by surprise. Two weeks ago our daughter Irene, who, while paranoid, had never done anything more violent than howl, suddenly swung the coffee table at me after I told her I was tired of her howling. I ducked and yelled. Some of the big boys caught her from behind and restrained her. But somewhere in the scuffle I broke a bone in my foot.

Some of our children are suicidal. We have no locks on either of our bathroom doors since bathrooms are often chosen as places to attempt self-destruction. We have learned to keep all sharp objects, even newly opened tin cans, out of the reach of such children.

It is hard for me to relax at night because there are so many things to watch, to listen for, to feel responsible about. And tonight we have a new son. His name is Eric. He is asleep in the TV room right now. A beautiful baby, with soft, cherubic lips, and long blond hair.

We had not meant to bring him home today, but the way it turned out, there was no choice. Moe and I both continue to see outpatients at the office to help support our family, and I was at the office when Moe asked me if I would take a look at this boy. It's amazing how the sick kids in a community all seem to know, and care, about each other. A couple of them had brought Eric to Moe a few days before and begged Moe to see him. "He's special," they told him. "You've got to do something about him before he gets locked up permanently."

Our house was full and Moe did not want to take a schizophrenic as an outpatient. He had agreed to evaluate the boy only in order to refer him to another therapist. He showed me test results. The boy looked very, very sick. Schizophrenic on the verge of regression.

When I walked into the office where he was waiting, Eric was sitting with his back to the door. When he heard my step, he rose, and looked at me with a half-smile. Tentative, hopeful, infinitely appealing.

"You're not afraid of me?" I asked, surprised.

"You're Moe's wife," he said simply. "I have to trust you."

I held out my hand. "Can I touch you?"

He nodded, his gaze intent.

I studied him carefully. There was something very strange about this boy. He was not behaving like a schizophrenic. He was not frightened of strangers. He did not mind being touched.

She doesn't frighten me. She could be my mother. I wish she'd be my mother. I've been searching for a mother since I was thirteen. But when she knows how bad I am, she won't want me!

His face did not have the flat, withdrawn affect typical of the schizophrenic. His expression was animated and lively. His blue eyes were bright with hope. He gestured freely when he spoke. His voice was low and urgent, and he seemed very eager to describe to me what a very bad boy he was and how terrified he was that he would kill someone. He also wanted me to know how sincerely, desperately he wanted help. "Just tell me what to do," he pleaded, "and I'll do it. Tell me anything and I'll do it!"

I don't want to hurt anyone. I don't want to kill anyone. But I'm so afraid I will. I tried to tell the psychiatrist how sick I am. But he just sat there smoking his pipe and asking questions. He didn't tell me what to do. He didn't tell me how I can keep from killing someone. Maybe she can tell me. She and Moe. They must help me!

Eric obviously felt that Moe and I were his one chance. He had been hospitalized a couple of times, had been picked up by the police, had jumped from a second story roof during a party, and during the previous week had had several "blackouts" following impulses to murder his girl friend and her children. Frantically seeking help, he found therapists who were unwilling to work with him. He assumed their rejection was because they recognized his intrinsic badness, because they knew he was hopelessly evil.

Since he seemed so alert and open, with none of the familiar withdrawal or apathy of the typical schizophrenic, I wondered if his illness might be physiological in origin. Perhaps a brain tumor. I excused myself and went in to check with Moe. "This kid is really strange," I told him. "I think you should get a neurological evaluation —"

"I already have," Moe said. "There is no organisity."

I wasn't sure what we should do, but I knew the boy should not be loose in the streets. Moe was needed at home and had to leave. I asked the boy to wait for me while I saw two patients— a young couple—who were friends of his. The young couple was arguing, and I realized that Eric could hear their voices from the waiting room, and might be frightened. My patients, also concerned, suggested that he might join us.

When I went out to get him, he had changed. A few moments earlier, his face had been childlike, open, his blue eyes soft and beseeching; now he was upset. The soft lines were drawing into a pale mask, the eyes were narrowing. One leg, crossed over the other, was jiggling. I glanced uneasily into Moe's office, but he had already gone home. When I asked Eric to join us, he followed me silently and sat down stiffly in the chair I indicated. As his two friends resumed their argument, he began to jiggle again. Now both legs were shaking. Then suddenly he bolted up and raced out the door.

I followed him. He had paused on the wooden porch which faces the street outside our office. I stood at a distance. He was motionless, but poised for flight. I hesitated to approach him, for fear of triggering the violence. My God, I thought, we'll end up with him racing through the streets with the police after him.

Then a car pulled to a stop in front of the office. John Christy, one of my sons-in-law, was at the wheel and he was never a more welcome sight. I drew him inside, explaining the problem. "See if you can get that kid off the porch." I backed off, to let John do the talking.

He walked quietly up to Eric. "You have to come inside," he said, his voice low, but firm.

Eric listened, apparently responding to the authority in John's voice, and docilely followed him back into Moe's office. I went to reassure my patients, then returned to Eric. He continued to look upset and I guessed it was John who was upsetting him now. I asked John to go call our oldest son, Aaron, to come and help. Aaron is big enough, strong enough, and shrewd enough to handle almost anyone. And Eric already knew him from school. Aaron was our first schizophrenic baby, the one we learned on. He is more knowledgeable about the disease than most trained psychiatrists. I hoped his presence would be less upsetting to Eric than that of a total stranger like John.

But as John left us, I suddenly realized what a foolish thing I had done. Now I was alone with this crazy boy. I was frightened. I didn't know who—or where or when—the violence would happen. But I knew it was coming. Somehow I must keep him under control.

"You can't let go here," I said. I have a very lightweight, squeaky child's voice and one of my constant problems is to make it sound authoritative enough to be effective.

He did not seem to have heard me. "In a few minutes Aaron will be here," I told him. "Aaron can take care of you."

I watched him, hoping the words would sink through, and put a brake on whatever was building up inside of him.

He did not answer. He was sitting silently, seething like a volcano about to erupt. He was not actually making any sound, but it was something I sensed, something I long ago learned to recognize. There is a lot of muscular tension. The body twitches. I could feel it and smell it. But there was no way I could judge how much time we had. Nor did I know what this boy would do. Outbursts of homicidal anger, like Elizabeth? Or a build-up, with plenty of signals put out to get help, like some of the others? If I were right in my hunch about this youngster, he would be like Elizabeth. I tried to establish visual contact but it was hopeless. His blue eyes were swimming out of focus.

I waited. It was nearly fifteen minutes by the office clock before Aaron's reassuring shadow filled the doorway. As he walked confidently into the room I felt the relief wash over me.

Aaron was absolutely great with the boy. He took in what was happening without any explanation from me, ambled across the room and put a friendly hand on Eric's shoulder. He spoke as one would when approaching a very timid young child for the first time. "Come on, baby, let's go home."

Eric rose obediently and glanced back at me as Aaron led him toward the door. He asked no questions about where he was going, why, or what was planned for him.

Aaron managed to get him home before he blew.

It was Moe who caught it. Aaron delivered Eric to Moe, and just a few moments later Eric suddenly left the room full of youngsters to whom he was being introduced and, despite a heavy rain, walked rapidly through the back door and toward the driveway. Moe went after him with Aaron following. Eric had already begun an episode that looked almost like convulsive seizures. His face was distorted into a vicious mask of terrible anger, bloody foam collected on lips drawn back from gnashing teeth. Unlike what would occur in convulsions, he struck out in a furiously purposeful way. Moe and Aaron could not hold him, and the three went down, a sprawled mass on the wet gravel. Altogether it took eight strong boys to restrain Eric until the upset was spent.

By the time I got home he was quiet, confused and frightened, and the boys were being checked for injuries. Eric had a sprained ankle and a lot of bruises, which he examined with a strange kind of clinical detachment. It was later I learned that Eric had a remarkable ability to deny pain, that he could discount the injuries almost completely.

I found pajamas and asked Aaron to clean him up while I spent some time reassuring the other boys. Moe called Dr. Reed, the director of the local mental hygiene clinic, who serves as our consultant, and asked him to make an emergency visit to prescribe for Eric, so that we would be able to put him safely to bed.

When he was finally cleaned up, sitting in the TV room in his pajamas, Eric could not remember what had happened. We described the episode to him, and as we talked I could see the fright and the confusion clearing up.

"You took care of me," he said, his lips trembling. "You didn't lock me up, you took care of me!" He looked around at us wonderingly, then at me.

"Am I an animal?" he asked. "Do you want me locked up?" As I reached out for him, he folded up, clinging to me.

"You're not an animal," I told him. "You're a little boy. A beautiful little boy!"

Later he lay relaxed in the makeshift bed we

set up for him, looking very vulnerable. The hard-faced twenty-one-year-old youth of the psychotic episode and the poised youngster I had seen at the office were both gone. His face was plump and soft, revealing the baby he really is; his lips were lax and full. As I tucked him in he clung to me, trying to tell me how ashamed and sorry he was about what he had done, trying to promise me that he would be good. "If I'm not," he said, in a little-boy lisp, " you can smack me down!"

Poor baby. How desperately he was trying to trade submission for protection against the terrible anger that is locked inside of him.

I kissed him goodnight, then left the door ajar to the next room, which several of the boys share, and I asked our son Bob to call me if he heard Eric stir.

I sleep only fitfully during the nighttime hours when we have a new baby in the house. We don't medicate our sick children heavily as they do in hospitals, and when they awaken in the middle of the night, they are apt to be upset. In the daylight, familiar surroundings and a secure structure can contain the craziness. At night, psychosis runs rampant. Often when I go to bed I mentally check out which children are most angry with me, and try to guess if there is any danger in falling asleep. Moe and I frequently sleep with a string of clattering chimes hung on our door to awaken us if anyone tries to come in.

When I came in from the office this evening and walked through the living room, it was like wading knee-deep in anger. As will often happen, one upset will trigger others, and nearly everyone was excited about what had happened with Eric. A lot of the hostility was coming from Barbara. I don't know why she was so angry and I was too busy with the new baby to find out.

Eric may want to kill me sometime, too. He is still too new, and has not yet transferred the anger he feels toward another mother to me. In many ways he reminds me of Aaron, when he first came to us. I thought how physically powerful and potentially dangerous he really is; my safety would depend on his need for mothering.

Moe is long since asleep and I am just beginning to doze when a tap awakens me. "Eric's awake and he's calling for you, Mom."

"All right," I whisper back, "bring him into the living room." I pull on my robe and limp out to the kitchen, closing the bedroom door carefully so as not to disturb Moe. In the kitchen I prepare a baby's bottle of warm milk sweetened with syrup and have it ready in the living room when Bob leads Eric in. He is stumbling sleepily, rubbing his eyes with one fist, but his color is bad, his face pale and fearful, and there is blood at the corner of his lips. I nod a silent thanks to Bob as he assists Eric onto the sofa and into my lap. The youngster folds all six feet of himself neatly against me.

"Hey, baby," I whisper, cradling his blond head on my arm. "Hey, little boy!" I hold the bottle to his lips so he can take some of the soothing warm milk, and as he sucks weakly I can feel him relax.

When he has taken what he wants, he is able to talk. "Bad dream," he mumbles, frightened, his voice that of a very young child. "Bad dreams woke me up." I stroke his blond hair back from his face as he tries to tell me. Both his skin and hair are damp from fright. "Baboons," he tells me. "Hundreds of baboons. And a clown —"

We shall find out what the baboons and clown mean tomorrow. "You're all right," I tell him now, continuing to stroke his head. "You're all right. You're my baby now and I'll take care of you."

He clutches the sleeve of my robe, his knuckles white with fear. "But if you know how bad I am you won't keep me," he whispers, searching my face with intense blue eyes.

"You're not a bad boy, Eric," I tell him. "You're a beautiful little boy. I love you."

"Will you say that again?" he asks, as he will undoubtedly ask again and again in months to come.

"I'm your mother now and I'll take care of you," I promise. "I love you."

Then, surprisingly, "You don't want me to be in a cage?" And, a moment later, "Am I a frog? Do you think I'm a frog?" So already we have begun the laborious process by which children— those who are healthy as well as those who are sick—find out who they are. "No, Eric. You're a boy, not a frog. Little boys aren't put in cages. You're a fine little boy."

Soon he is ready to fall asleep in my arms, Bob

and I get him to bed once more, and I return to my own room.

As I open the door softly I can see the gray morning light at the window. It is now past five o'clock. I slip back into bed beside Moe, marveling that he can sleep so soundly. I touch his arm and he stirs and reaches out for me. I am glad he is still asleep. There is a lot for him to do tomorrow.

He is Eric's father now. He became the boy's father in the first few moments they spent together. Just as he became Aaron's father three years ago when we took our first schizophrenic baby.

Chapter Two

MOE AND I ARRIVED at our present work by very different routes. The similar thread that ran through both of our earlier lives and shaped the life we now share is, of course, our investment in children. Healthy children and sick children who should have the chance to become healthy.

Polish Jews, Moe's family emigrated to the United States when he was ten years old and settled in Virginia. His father was fortunate in making a good deal of money quickly in this country, in the restaurant and grocery business, and Moe followed him in the family businesses for nearly twenty years before he decided what he really wanted to do was work with children.

Although he had been married before we met, he had had no children. So he decided to become a psychiatric social worker and devote himself to the care of disturbed youngsters. At thirty-seven he retired from business life and enrolled in college. When I met him in graduate school he was one year short of finishing his master's degree in social work.

I reached Virginia quite by chance. My people are Scandinavians who settled on the West Coast, and I was born in the mill and fishing town of Everett, Washington, about forty miles north of Seattle. On the face of it, my childhood appears confused. My parents were teenagers who eloped, conceived me, and never really established a home together. My mother was little more than a child herself at the time of my birth, and pretty much turned me over to my maternal grandmother to raise. I was brought up by two grandmothers who, fortunately, shared a talent for mothering. It is not unusual among Scandinavians for established households to raise children who need a home either because the mother has died, or is ill, or is simply too young, as was my case. And so I grew up with the idea that adopted and foster children were as well loved and cared for as natural children.

In addition to my grandmothers, the other major influence on my life was the man who was a father to me, my mother's second husband, a big, strong, very masculine man of Icelandic extraction, who was a juvenile officer and is presently the chief of police in Everett. He always had a lot of kids around him, mostly boys who were in trouble, and I was impressed with the fact that he was very authoritarian, a strict disciplinarian, and yet he earned and kept the boys' affection and respect.

In Transactional Analysis, the theorectical framework we use in treating our sick children, we are very concerned with what children learn from their parents. The whole Parent Ego State is incorporated as an imitation of the parents or other parental figures. In addition, the Child Ego State takes in parental messages which we call "script"; the script includes descriptions of who and what the child will become and how he will go about doing things. All of our children incorporated a sick Parent Ego State and a self-destructive script from their natural parents. The process we call "Reparenting" involves erasing the Parent Ego State completely, a procedure easily done with schizophrenics. It is more difficult to get at the sick script, but that, too, must be replaced with healthy messages about the child's self, what the world is like and what he will do in the world.

The principal message I incorporated from my father was: *"You're a damn smart kid. You can do anything you want to do!"* Recently a friend asked me where I ever got "permission" to do the things he had seen me attempt, and I knew that it had come from that parental message. My father's belief in my being able to do unusual things gave me the confidence to try to treat patients whom other therapists considered untreatable. I have felt unusually free to pursue unexplored areas in my field, and both develop and test my own theories with minimal concern for tradition.

Although my father influenced my development tremendously, and I still feel enormous respect and affection for him, the independence he taught me caused a rift in our relationship. As I grew older, many of my values differed from his. Moreover, he was disappointed at my unwillingness to settle down in Everett. I think he had no idea of the magnitude of the ambition he fostered in me, my need to explore the resources of the world around me.

I left Everett at seventeen to go to the University of Washington, very much to my family's distress. However, by then my father's messages about being independent had taken root.

The university, unfortunately, was not nearly so stimulating or challenging as I had hoped. I attended classes at random without bothering to work toward a degree; I dabbled with a direct mail business and an advertising agency of my own; and I married a psychology student. I was eager to have children, and when my first baby, a little girl whom we christened Vikki, suffered a lung collapse and died three months after her birth, I got pregnant again as soon as possible. I lost that child in a miscarriage and doctors told me that it seemed likely there was a genetic problem which might mean I could not have healthy babies.

It was very important for me to have children and very frightening when I thought I might not be able to. From seven pregnancies I managed to have three living children: my sons Chucky, Tom, and Rickey. By then my husband and I were living in San Francisco and, while I at long last had achieved the family I desired, my marriage itself was in trouble. My husband came from a wealthy family and when he began having difficulty with his vision, he decided to withdraw from professional life and simply live on family money.

I could not have agreed less on a way of life.

When it was obvious that I had no intention

of sharing his passive way of life, my husband and I divorced: and I took full responsibility for our three small boys.

By now I was actively involved in social welfare work for the county, and I had also begun working with the San Francisco Seminar, a group of therapists, led by Dr. Eric Berne, who were responsible for the development of Transactional Analysis as a method of treatment. Dr. Berne was later to popularize this method in *Games People Play*. The TA method of dividing the personality into Adult, Parent and Child Ego States, is an excellent way of diagnosing, analyzing and attempting to resolve psychiatric problems. It appealed to me as a far more efficient, comprehensive, and vigorous approach to mental illness than traditional methods of treatment. I was excited by a method that held out a real solution of problems, instead of merely mirroring them.

The years that I was active with the Seminar in San Francisco gave me professional encouragement for my own ideas and served to reinforce that expectation that I would demonstrate that I was indeed a very bright child. That it was the Child within me that was to do something important seems very significant to me. The message from my father, "You are a bright kid," left open the freedom, creativity, and energetic resources of my Child Ego State. The Child is the most "real self" as well as the strongest part of the personality. It is responsible for feelings, biological needs, motivation, and expressiveness. It is the child at two, and at four, and at ten, with all the daring and spontaneity of those early years. My Child is very much the little professor. She gets excited by ideas; big, important ideas. She is fascinated with the possibility that somewhere, floating around in a kind of idea limbo are thoughts, possibilities and ways of doing things which have not yet been captured and cultivated. That somewhere in primitive man, if only we can clear out a lot of the cultural garbage that intercedes between who he is and who we are, lie the resources for solving all the important problems that confront people.

So why not cure schizophrenia? There are many big problems in the world that I have thought about. But somewhere, sometime, I decided that I was going to solve the problem of schizophrenia, that I would find out what happens inside of the million or more people (in this country alone) who struggle with the disease, and almost inevitably lose the struggle and that I was going to be the resource through which at least some of them would get well.

The San Francisco Seminar gave me the encouragement to expound and work out my theories, and it was there also that I learned the power of group therapy and discovered my own talent for it. I am far more effective working in groups than with individuals, since the group tends to heighten my perceptions.

But I soon began to realize that if I were to develop my theories through work as a practicing therapist, I needed to go back and pick up the academic degrees that I had failed to get when I was in college. The welfare department for which I worked offered to send me to graduate school in exchange for a contract which would require that I come back and work for them. Since I was not certain that I wanted to work indefinitely in the county—or in the state of California, for that matter—I applied elsewhere for scholarships in mental health, and was accepted by William and Mary College in Virginia (now the Virginia Commonwealth University).

Moe and I met, at a graduate school picnic, three days after my little boys and I reached Richmond. Until then I would have laughed at anyone who used the phrase "love at first sight." But it happened to Moe and me.

From entirely different backgrounds, living on opposite sides of the continent, we had each independently been developing our lives along the same lines. We thought the same way, and we felt the same way about nearly everything from politics to child care. Doers by disposition, we had each been actively involved in the civil rights movement in our areas. Both of us basically believed in the "allrightness" of people, and in the right of people to have feelings and to express those feelings; the right of people to have needs. Professionally we were each concerned with getting our academic degrees behind us in order to be able to work with, and hopefully find cures for, emotionally disturbed children.

One of the nicest things about Moe was his obvious attraction to my three sons. There were moments when I thought he might even care more about becoming their father than he cared about his relationship with me.

Now I know that Moe is instinctively attracted to all children who need fathering, he is a marvelous, natural father: committed, intelligent, and infinitely loving.

An outspoken, outgoing, genuinely emotional man, one of the ways that Moe has of expressing his feelings is to touch people. If a child seems distressed or frightened, he automatically pulls him onto his lap or gives him a warm reassuring bear hug. It is Moe's nature to do this.

Not long after we met, Moe, as a student therapist in training (he was one year ahead of me in school), was assigned to treat an eight-year-old boy. At first the child was hostile, negativistic, and arguing about everything. When Moe attempted to relate to him, using traditional play therapy methods, working with darts and other games, the boy played "Schlemiel" and did everything wrong. Moe was patient, however, and finally the boy relinquished his hostility enough to allow Moe to teach him to play a game well. The day he performed beautifully and made a perfect score, Moe snatched him up and hugged him, then held him on his lap for a few moments telling him how proud he was of his accomplishment. All of this he dutifully recorded in his notes. When his supervisor read them she was horrified. "You're not supposed to touch patients," she scolded. "Why, the boy might think it was a homosexual advance!"

Moe went right on touching the child since he sensed what is true of so many sick children, that the boy was starved for affection. From the day that Moe hugged the boy, the child's attitude changed. He quit fighting Moe, and worked hard to get well.

This was yet another point on which Moe and I agreed: In times of stress there is nothing so reassuring as an arm around the shoulder, or the touch of someone's hand. We both consider this an "all right" human need, one that none of us outgrows.

In Transactional Analysis we refer to all comforting, constructive or supportive gestures, communicated either verbally or by touching, as "strokes." The need for stroking is experienced by all of us, and is crucial for children's survival and development. Another important attitude we emphasize is "I'm okay-you're okay." Much traditional treatment focuses on the patient as a not-okay person, which justifies the therapist acting as detached and superior. Although we do not all engage in touch-stroking, all TA therapists recognize the basic okayness of people, whether or not they are patients, and believe this is necessary in creating a climate where getting well is possible.

Moe was impressed with my description of the means by which TA therapists relate to their patients. He finished his degree, a year ahead of me, and was working at a center for the treatment of delinquent children in North Carolina, when I got an urgent letter from him. "I can't communicate with these kids. Please send TA pamphlets."

Moe started using TA methods as soon as he

received my reply. It was amazing to him, how swiftly kids are able to pick up and use the concept of Parent, Adult and Child Ego States. When they are told that we each have a moralizing, nurturing Parent; a problem-solving, data-processing Adult; and an emotional, powerful Child it provides them an easy way to sort out their ideas and feelings. Most children find it easy to understand that the Child has two faces: the Natural Child which reacts spontaneously, and the Adapted Child, who may look "sweet and good" or be angry and rebellious, but is reacting to authority figures. Adapting is a game which children learn to play very early, in order to get what their Natural Child really needs and wants.

When I completed my degree I got a job doing medical social work for handicapped children at the University Hospital in Charlottesville, Virginia, but soon resigned that in favor of dividing my time between rural clinics and private practice. Moe was by now working in a mental health clinic in Charlottesville, and we married and settled there. At that time we had no thoughts of taking sick children into our home.

Then I met Aaron.

His name was not Aaron in those days. (Aaron was the name we selected later for his new, healthy self.) His name was Dennis. His fellow students at the University of Virginia called him "Jesus."

Dennis was a rather notorious figure around Charlottesville—a tall, thin boy with long, dirty-blond hair and a full, unkempt beard, who walked with the stiff, forward tilt of the paranoid. His clothes, which were so filthy they were literally rotting off him, consisted of ragged jeans, an ancient Boy Scout shirt, and a floppy black hat. He was seldom seen without a knapsack on his back (guesses about its contents ranged from bread and wine to drugs and ammunition) and a crooked, rum-soaked cigar in his mouth. He also, we learned later, was never far from his small arsenal of guns and knives. He would not have considered walking on the street without a weapon of some kind, and he slept with a loaded .38 revolver six inches from his head. He hung around with a handful of other sick youngsters, in a partially deserted, forbidding-looking, ante-bellum mansion which was locally known as the "ghost house." Dennis was a grotesque and familiar figure at all rallies and meetings, and something of a political activist. I had once spoken to a student group of which he was a member and he had demonstrated open hostility toward me and made derogatory remarks about social workers.

A college friend of his called me during the summer of 1966, and asked if I would see Dennis, who, in his opinion, had become an emergency case. When I agreed to see him, the boy brought Dennis to our house, where I maintained my office.

Dennis had deteriorated noticeably from the time I had seen him, a few months earlier. At nineteen he looked thirty-five. His long thin face was twisted into hard, angry lines. His mouth hung loose and dripped saliva. His long, matted, dirty hair and beard were caked with scaly dandruff. And while I have observed that schizophrenics have a distinct odor, Dennis plainly stank. It did not take much time in diagnosis to establish that he was paranoid, delusional, homicidal—and dangerous.

I carefully kept the coffee table between us while we talked, wondering how anyone that sick, that frightened and that threatening could still be walking around on the streets. He had been receiving treatment of sorts at the University clinic for the past six months and had been hospitalized after swallowing a bottle of aspirin. His activities recently included chasing his fellow students with a saber, and cutting off a piece of his finger and presenting it to a friend.

The doctor wouldn't tell me how sick I am. But I've got it figured out. I'm paranoid. Who else but a paranoid thinks everyone is watching him? When I walk down the street I think all the people I see are staring at me and whispering about me. I put my hand on the knife in my pocket to reassure myself. It's a big knife with a long blade which I keep very sharp.

I am afraid all the time. I am overwhelmed with fear. The fear is so great that I feel like attacking. But I don't want to kill anyone. It's better if I kill myself....

The suicide attempt was Dennis's desperate cry for help, the cry that so many schizophrenics make when they are still hoping that somehow, somewhere, within the great medical structure, there is some kind of salvation for them. But what Dennis had found is what most psychotics find: that the kind of help that is available does not have the resources or the understanding to give him what he needs, to resolve the fearful conflict which is already invading his perceptions. The hospital structure frightened and confused Dennis. It defined him and his needs as "not-okay." The therapist who was assigned to him was too afraid of the possibility of violence to see Dennis alone. He was always interviewed by the doctor in the presence of burly medical students.

Dennis knew he was sick. He knew he needed help. But he did not know which way to turn. I was amazed that despite his mental and physical deterioration and his rapidly fading contact with reality, he still had a powerful, driving urge for survival. He not only wanted to live. He wanted to and, despite the evidence against him, really believed that he could get well.

I'm sure she can help me. I've been looking for help for so long and this is the first time anyone has shown me that they know what I need. It's such a relief to have someone agree that I am sick. When I told my friend the minister he kept saying, 'You are perfectly normal—maybe just a little bit mixed up.' He thinks it's important for the preservation of left wing politics on the campus that I am not crazy, and that I stay active....

I am afraid that I will kill someone soon and I will be locked up.

As Dennis spoke to me about his frustrations in trying to get help, told me his own version of what was wrong with him, admitted the frightening likelihood that he would kill someone soon, I realized that the chances of successfully treating this boy as an outpatient were very slim. He was already so sick that my even offering to help him seemed a kind of fraud.

How do you tell a boy that he is going to die? Death as an end to misery is one thing. The death that I envisioned for him was sixty years entombed in the back ward of a hospital. Because once he acted out his violence in a homicidal way, he would be locked into a psychiatric ward for life.

I kept thinking, as I sat and watched this grotesque youth, twitching, filthy, mouthing violence and obscenities, that somewhere beneath all that dirt and sickness was a nineteen-year-old boy! Somewhere else was the deprived child, still lingering in those dreadful moments of fear and need when all this began.

When I checked with the resident at the hospital who had seen Dennis, he told me that he was not interested in treating the patient—whom he considered dangerous. The prognosis, in his estimation, was completely negative. He warned me never to see Dennis alone. Both he and the staff doctor—to whom I also spoke—confirmed that Dennis was clearly a paranoid schizophrenic.

Before he left my office that day Dennis agreed to keep his appointments regularly. I also insisted that he join a group therapy session I conducted once a week which was composed of university students. He was reluctant to do this, but at my insistence he finally consented.

I was surprised at how responsible Dennis was about keeping his appointments with me. Too frightened to cope with buses or taxicabs, he walked the several miles from the campus to my house. Usually he was early. When he appeared on our street, I noticed that some of my neighbors watched him covertly. There were no hippies in those days, and few beatniks in Virginia. Dennis was so bizarre in his appearance that even walking down the street he was threatening to many conservative citizens.

The course of treatment was relatively uneventful for several weeks. I stood off, afraid to offer much, shamefully aware of my own limitations. I was aware also that time was running out for Dennis. There were a few isolated moments of progress, however. And I could feel his excitement when he was able to make me understand something that was happening inside of him.

The one thing Dennis completely blanked out on was his mother. He was either unable or unwilling to supply information about her. He insisted that he could not remember her. He could not describe what she looked like. The only thing he could tell me was her schedule—at what times she went to work, came home, and so forth.

I was surprised at the group's interest and investment in Dennis, considering his behavior to them. He never responded to anyone; never looked directly at anyone; stared constantly at his own knee throughout the weekly sessions. He rarely volunteered anything, and if the boys got angry with him, he accepted the hostility passively. But as the group continued to show its interest in and concern for him, he began to accept its authority. On the group's advice—and its members were all young fellow students— he began to see less of the crowd of sick, drug-oriented homosexuals he had been associating with. He also clearly made an effort, at the suggestion of the group, to control his hallucinations. These were suggestions he could accept from his peers—although he refused to accept similar admonitions from me. He remained negative toward me without being overtly hostile.

I continued to see Dennis alone—despite the hospital therapist's warning—but I was afraid to touch him. Most therapists at that time, including myself, had been schooled never to touch a paranoid, for fear you might precipitate something terrible. Now I know that this is not always true. But it was something which both Dennis and I had to learn together.

Dennis had been in private treatment with me, and attending the weekly group, for nearly six months with small moments of hope but no significant improvement when, one Friday night, he went into a spontaneous fantasy for the first time. In the fantasy he was being flogged by his father. He was very upset afterward, and I made an appointment for him to come and see me the next day.

On Saturday, when we were alone and I asked him to repeat it, the fantasy changed. This time

Dennis was about six years old, and it was he who was flogging his father. His father was lying naked on the floor. The mother was present, but disinterested. Dennis was begging his mother to intervene and protect him from his aggressive behavior toward his father, but she refused.

Obviously this fantasy was very significant to Dennis because in acting it out he became very agitated. "Look out!" he warned me suddenly. "Something's going to happen. Get help!"

"Nothing can happen until you tell me what it means," I told him, trying to sound calm.

He told me that when he was six or seven years old he was sitting on the edge of his mother's bed and his father came in and cuffed him and told him to stay away from his mother.

As he described the scene, Dennis began to shake so violently that the couch he was sitting on rattled.

"You better get help!" he cried out to me. "Something's going to happen!"

"You're not going to do anything now, Dennis," I told him firmly. "You are going to wait until I can get someone here so that both you and I will be protected. You are not going to do anything until we both are safe."

I was excited—and more than a little frightened. Obviously we had touched upon a significant aspect of Dennis's pathology and he was on the verge of a psychotic episode of some sort. When this state is reached in a hospital situation or with a psychiatrist, the patient is either encouraged to suppress it or he is tranquilized to the point that he cannot act. I felt, however, that if we could take a look at the psychosis, it might furnish a clue as to what Dennis needed to get well.

But if I did let Dennis act out whatever was boiling inside of him, I did not know what we would have on our hands. Although their basic energizing force is fear, a paranoid usually attempts to bypass that fear by shifting his energy into pathological (frequently homicidal) anger.

I called Moe who was at his office downtown, and told him to hurry home.

Moe had met Dennis several times at the house when the boy was waiting to see me. But Moe had been unable to relate to him. Most of this stemmed from the fact that Dennis always seemed very afraid of Moe, and avoided any contact.

When Moe walked into the office where Dennis and I were waiting for him, Dennis shrank with terror. "I didn't mean anything," he whimpered. "I wasn't going to do anything to her—"

"Don't worry, son," Moe said, "I won't let you hurt her."

"I hate her! I hate her!" Dennis cried out suddenly, explosively. "She's a goddam bitch! I hate all women!"

He leaped up and started for the window.

"Sit down and behave yourself!" Moe shouted at him. Dennis stopped, dead still, then turned back to the couch and sat down. He was shaking very hard.

Moe waited for me to do something, and I began cautiously. "Dennis thinks there is a line between himself and the rest of the world," I explained. "He believes that everything on his side of the line is real, and that everything beyond the line is unreal." I turned to Dennis. "What would you do if I came inside the line?"

Dennis shook even harder and began gasping for breath.

I walked over to where he sat on the couch. "I won't touch you," I promised him. "But you can touch me." I held out my hand.

"Oh no, no please, please, I can't!" Dennis shrank back against the couch.

"Why not?"

"If I touched you, you'd be real!"

"What will you do if I sit down beside you?"

"I'll jump out the window."

"Try to tell us why you are so afraid, son," Moe urged the boy. "Why are you so afraid to touch her?"

I sat down beside him. Dennis just shook his head violently, his mouth open, gasping for air like a newly landed trout.

"Dennis," I said, still extending my hand, "if you needed help, who would you go to?"

"To him," Dennis gasped in a strangled voice, nodding toward Moe.

"If you trust me, son," Moe told him, "then you must believe me when I say that it is safe for you to turn to her. Do what you need to do, son."

By now Dennis was shaking so hard his teeth were rattling and he was sobbing. Suddenly his arm whipped out—I thought at first to strike me—and he snatched hold of my hand.

When he touched me, he stopped shaking and

sobbing. He stared at my hand in a very puzzled way.

"Am I real, Dennis?" I asked him.

"No," he said, "only your hand is real."

"What is it you want, son?" Moe pressed him gently.

Without another word, Dennis very quietly assumed a fetal position, cuddled into my lap, and attempted to nurse.

We stared at him in astonishment. Both of us had been prepared for an outbreak of terrible anger. But Dennis's face was serene. Despite the beard, it was clearly the face of a baby of about nine months of age, a nursing infant. His body, all six feet two inches of it, was uncoordinated, just as an infant's is before it gains muscular control. I recognized from my experience with my own babies the movements he was making with his mouth and tongue, curling his tongue as though around a nipple. An adult can't do it. Only a nursing baby can. Or a regressed schizophrenic.

When Moe attempted to pull the big boy off my lap, Dennis began to cry. But not as he had cried before out of adolescent terror. Now the cry was that of a very young baby—that uninflected howl an infant makes before it has learned to use its cry to mean anything more than a sustained demand for care. He was too young for real tears. A single drop formed on his long lashes, then slid slowly down his cheek.

Moe and I looked at each other over the boy's head. It was at that moment that we fell in love with this child and silently committed ourselves to his care.

"So I guess he'll stay," I said.

We watched for nearly an hour while Dennis contentedly fell asleep in my arms.

I had thought a great deal about re-parenting as a method of treatment for curing schizophrenics. But, until I held that big suckling boy in my arms, I had not really thought about becoming the patient's mother.

Chapter Three

I HAD NEVER SEEN a patient right at the time of regression before I held Dennis in my arms. The thing that struck me most forcibly was that he did not "feel crazy" at all. His body, which in all my previous contact with him had been rigid, angry, old beyond his years, was now limp, relaxed, and peaceful. As I watched his serene slumber I thought of the haunted, sleepless nights he had described to me, of the constant suffering he had experienced which had been so little relieved by my efforts at conventional therapeutic methods.

The Parent within me, especially that part of my Parent incorporated from the psychotherapeutic community, preached caution: It said that what I was doing was unprofessional, that therapists did not nurture patients.

But there I was, with a paranoid boy who believed that I could show him the way to get well, and with the Child within me, who believed in the magic of solving problems, urging me to accept the challenge.

As I caressed his cheek, I wondered just how I could care for him. Since regression is usually discouraged, there were no guidelines. Would this infantile state last long? Or might Dennis suddenly erupt into violent, crazy behavior which I would be unable to handle?

On the face of it, it seemed impractical to even try to manage a six-foot infant. Could he walk? Go to the bathroom by himself? Eat with a fork? What would happen when some conflict arose between us? Would he react as an infant—or as a pathological, full-grown man?

If we did let Dennis be a child again, what sort of child would we be dealing with? I knew that Dennis's own Natural Child, deprived long ago of the nurturing he had needed, was not a healthy child. He was sick, angry, frightened about the terrifying things that went on in his head, bitter about the parenting which had so miserably failed him, furious at having incorporated a Parent Ego State which had proved hostile to him, locking him into a state of suffering from which he could not escape—except into infancy. I wondered what would happen when he transferred to Moe and me all the hatred he felt for his own parents. Could we possibly build a relationship quick enough and secure enough to get us all safely through it?

Although it was three years before we understood the full significance of the fantasy which had triggered Dennis's regression, we worked out that it must have been about separation from his mother. When Dennis was eleven months old, a younger sister was born. Dennis experienced his mother's hospitalization and return home with a new baby as abandonment. He reacted by rejecting both her and the baby. His mother, perhaps overwhelmed by two such young infants so close together, gave Dennis over to the complete care of his father. Dennis's father was physically handicapped and had a serious psychiatric problem. He was ill fitted to the role of nurturing parent and Dennis grew up terrorized by a father whom he both loved and hated, urgently longing for the mothering he never received, but perceiving his mother as his father's wife, having little or no relationship to himself.

As a child grows up, he incorporates innumerable messages about himself and the world around him from his parents, which then become part of his own Parent Ego State. Dennis's experience as a child led him to believe that his mother was cold and rejecting, that she favored girl children (his younger sister), and that she was unable to take a stand against his domineering father. His father was an alcoholic whom Dennis also believed to be homicidal and brutal. The result of all this was that Dennis defined himself and the world around him with three positive messages: "I'm not-okay" (my mother doesn't like me); "Parents come first" (in any conflict between what Dennis had wanted or needed and what his parents had wanted, his own wishes had been ignored); "The world is a bad place" (his parents' conversation usually centered around evil people, evil deeds and their own isolation from society—a gambit which in TA parlance is known as playing the game Ain't It Awful).

Later we were to discover that these three parental messages are to be found present in all schizophrenics. As soon as one of them can be eliminated, the patient can begin to get well.

In the San Francisco Seminar when we had discussed the three ego states, Parent, Child and Adult, it had not made sense to me that the Parent part of the personality was considered permanent and inflexible. After all, we do change our values even in late maturity. I argued then, albeit somewhat timidly, that any structure which was derived from one's environment (outside oneself) in imitation of others (parents or parent-figures) could perhaps be destroyed and re-established. If a sick child's Parent was based on misperceptions of himself and the world, why not erase those sick messages and substitute a healthy set in their place? I was told, at the time, that the impact of the original parent-child relationship was inescapable and that the closest anyone had ever come to restructuring a personality was through psychoanalysis.

But I still believed that the Parent could be restructured through therapy based on reparenting the Child. The principal characteristics of schizophrenia are behavior that is inappropriate to the event, mental confusion, and regression. It seemed likely to me that the key to curing the illness might lie in the patient's tendency to regress. Regression, known to be a re-enactment of childhood, is considered "crazy" or pathological and discouraged in conventional treatment because neither therapists nor mental hospitals are prepared to handle infants. A child needs, above all else, a mother. He must be held and stroked, fed and bathed, and loved. He needs a healthy family with two responsible parents.

If the schizophrenic patient regresses and then grows up again, I thought it possible that this would give him the opportunity to discard former concepts and rebuild new ones. What I was proposing to attempt with Dennis involved a total rebuilding of his personality, exposing his Child to an entirely new parental and societal experience, on the assumption that he would then have a choice between a pathological and a healthier personality structure.

After making sure that Dennis could not continue to care for himself, I talked to him about the possibility of his coming to stay with us and about my ideas of reparenting. I could not be sure how much he understood of what I was saying, but his relief at being assured of parenting was enormous. If he could be a baby and get cared for and stroked at home he was convinced he could use the Adult part of his personality and behave appropriately at other times.

When I told Dennis that he was to move into our house and become a member of our family, he displayed neither surprise nor gratitude. He appeared to take for granted that I should care for him since he had decided I was his mother. The question in his mind seemed to be more whether I would follow through on my responsibilities. When I tried to explain to him that what we were going to attempt would be highly experimental and unconventional, he turned away from me abruptly, obviously unwilling to consider the possibility that we might fail.

I feel so different, so fresh and young again, I know what they are doing is right. They cannot fail with me. I believe I can get well.

Moe and I thought that it was important for Dennis to maintain some semblance of normal grown-up behavior, and we discounted his efforts to communicate his need to be totally a baby. I realize now that this resulted from our anxiety and was contradictory to Dennis's best interests. My attempts to explain the experimental and unconventional aspects of what we were doing was also an attempt on my part to get the sick boy to assume some responsibility for our uncertainty—at a time when he could not afford to consider the possibility that he would not get well.

The day he brought his belongings to our house and moved into our guest room, Dennis arrived with his arsenal of weapons which Moe, with an outraged glance at me, quickly and efficiently confiscated. Poor Moe! I had forgotten to warn him about the guns and knives. Dennis seemed quite impressed with the authoritative way Moe took his weapons away from him, and he surrendered them quite docilely. He was anxious to communicate to us what a "bad" child he was and it was obviously a relief to him to know his access to destructive implements would be controlled and to be assured that it was unnecessary for him to protect himself, a different message than he had gotten in his natural family where weapons were constantly at hand.

"You are our child now," I told him. "No one wants to hurt you. We will take care of you."

As soon as we sat down to family dinner with our new child we realized we could not eat at the same table with him without doing something about his table manners. Dennis told us that his own family had rarely shared regular meals, and he seemed to have been given no information about appropriate table behavior. He grew sullen and angry when I demanded good table manners and he was critical of my cooking. Eating with Dennis obviously was not going to be a joy. What I did not realize was that table manners were as yet an unreasonable demand to make on him. In his regression Dennis was not actually old enough to sit at the table and feed himself. His unpleasant behavior was the result of not being able to meet my expectations.

We were not sure just what age he was. In my arms he had appeared around nine months, and he ranged from that to about three years of age, judging by his physical coordination. He was very clinging with me and extremely pleased to be allowed to come into our bedroom. At first, if he came in and found Moe was there, Dennis was frightened. But, after repeated reassurance from Moe that it was "all right" for him to come in, Dennis trailed me whenever he wanted to. He referred to me as "Mommy" and he lisped a great deal. It seemed very important to him that I put him to bed at night and he would stay awake until I came in to tuck him in and kiss him.

As soon as he was settled with us, we started to change his freakish appearance. When Moe told him he would have to take a shower every day, Dennis, somewhat to our surprise, put up no resistance. But when Moe also told him he would have to give up the filthy outfit he habitually wore and put on clean clothing every day, he was indignant. He hotly defended his rotting wardrobe and his right to be dirty.

After a lengthy, loud harangue, which accomplished nothing, Moe had had enough. "You put on those clothes right this minute," he thundered at Dennis, "or—I'll spank you!"

I knew, from the way that Moe was overacting, just how scared he was at the prospect of having to make good his threat.

But Dennis, who is actually an inch or two taller than Moe, cowered before his new "Daddy," looked very frightened and respectful, stopped arguing, and meekly put on the clean clothes.

We both breathed a private sigh of relief. It was a reaction that Moe was counting on—but neither one of us had had enough experience with regression to be assured that it would work out like that.

We soon learned that it was pointless to try to reason with our new child. Dennis automatically discounted all logical argument. He did not respond to explanations. He did respond, however, to authority.

His hair and beard posed another problem. We finally persuaded him to get his hair trimmed but he got hysterical if we even mentioned doing away with his beard. I already knew from our previous sessions that the beard represented much pathology for Dennis. First of all, it identified him with his natural father, who was bearded. It also reinforced his thinking of himself as "different" from other people. And when his appearance attracted critical stares in public it verified his sick perception of the world as a hostile, scary place. Because of his violent resistance we decided not to make an immediate issue of his appearance—a decision which the three of us were later to regret.

In addition to the rest of his disreputable appearance, Dennis had what looked to me like one of the worst cases of dandruff I had ever seen. His entire scalp was covered with open sores and a crusty scab. He told me that he had always had dandruff and was insistent that it did not improve with any kind of home treatment. After several unsuccessful attempts to persuade him to go alone to a dermatologist, I finally undertook to take him to the doctor myself.

This was my first experience in taking a regressed child out into the world of grown-up expectations.

I first telephoned the doctor's office and explained to the nurse that I was bringing a young man in who had a psychiatric problem and was quite immature in his behavior. She was reassuring and promised to explain the situation to the doctor.

Dennis seemed very frightened and apprehensive the day of the appointment. By the time we arrived at the doctor's waiting room, he was half-crying and drooling, clinging to me, and trying to hide behind me—which was something of a feat, considering the fact that he is a good foot taller than I am. The nurse, after a distressed moment, hurried us on into an examining room, away from the view of other patients.

The doctor appeared almost immediately. Dennis cried and clung to me.

"Mommy, will it hurt?"

The doctor was obviously disconcerted. I noticed Dennis watching him slyly, then he relaxed when he saw how up-tight the doctor really was, and began to enjoy himself. As I was to learn later, Dennis really did like to frighten people. He puffed himself up to look bigger and fiercer than he was, then talked deliberately exaggerated baby talk, gleefully watching the doctor, and me, as he did it.

I enjoy scaring people. It makes me laugh inside to see how frightened people are of me!

Then he calmed down, and became interested in the procedure when the doctor began examining him.

What I had assumed was just bad dandruff actually turned out to be something quite different, a rash from which Dennis had probably suffered since birth. The doctor assured us that it was not uncommon and not difficult to treat, but that it was a chronic problem and would require regular care. He seemed surprised that a condition of that sort had not been recognized, diagnosed, and properly treated long before.

Dennis left the doctor's office obviously pleased. I didn't realize just how important the visit was for him until months later, long after he was a big boy, when he still sought my assistance in caring for the rash. The fact that I had noticed the problem and done something about it seemed very significant to him. It meant, to Dennis, that we really were willing to take care of him and provide him with the attention that his natural parents had failed to offer him.

We assumed, when Dennis first came to us, that we were in for a lot of "crazy" behavior. To our surprise, once his infantile needs were met, and he felt cared for and loved, he voluntarily relinquished much of his pathological behavior. Later, we were to discover this same ability in the other sick children, which made it easier for us to live as a family. When a child acts "crazy" or "pathy," the other children discourage the behavior or call it to the attention of the household in a family group.

We are an authoritarian family and we did not ask our own children's consent when we brought Dennis into the house. At this time the two younger boys, nine-year-old Tom and six-year-old Rickey, were at home. Our oldest son, Chucky, who was eleven, had been seriously ill with encephalitis, and was then in a special school program on the West Coast. He was due home the following summer.

We had tried to prepare Tom and Rickey for Dennis's arrival but it was difficult since we ourselves did not actually know what to expect from our new child. Neither of the boys seemed upset or jealous of Dennis, however, and in a sense it was easier for them to accept him as an infant and a family member than it was for us.

Tom is a warm, sensitive boy, big for his age,

slow of movement and speech, with an unusual amount of self-confidence. He does not allow himself to be pushed or used and reacts to anything he considers unreasonable with stubborn refusal. He also, we soon learned, has a remarkable awareness of pathology and seemed instinctively to understand some behavior which mystified us.

Tom watched Dennis for a few days, then explained to his younger brother, "Oh, he's a baby," and Tom began to relate to Dennis on that level, as though he, Tom, were the older boy. He was willing to play with Dennis, to help take care of him, and to make friends without any apparent prejudice against mental illness.

Rickey had a more difficult adjustment to make to his new brother. The opposite of easygoing, slow-moving Tom, Rickey is quick, competitive, changeable in mood. He attacks the world with enthusiastic vigor and reacts with indignation when it does not meet his expectations. He was willing to play with Dennis and to share his toys with him so long as Dennis behaved in a normal fashion. But Rickey made it clear that he did not like crazy or strange behavior.

Dennis's attitude to the two boys was somewhat ambivalent. On the one hand he was jealous of the attention I paid to them, and on the other he sought their friendship. He had been with us a few days when I came home one afternoon to find the kitchen in a mess, the result of some boyish concoction.

"Who left the kitchen like this?" I demanded angrily. "Who didn't clean up after himself?"

There was the usual long, guilty silence. And then Dennis spoke up.

"I did it."

"You did not!" Tom said furiously. "I made that mess and you know I did! I don't know what you're trying to do, but mind your own business!"

"But I thought you'd like me if I took the blame for you—" Dennis faltered. He was obviously frightened by Tom's anger—and also perplexed.

"That's no way to make friends," Tom told him. "I don't want a friendship that's based on lies!"

Tom's ethics were more than Dennis was prepared to handle at the moment. But after that confrontation, he related to Tom with respect, and was even willing to accept Tom's authority when we were not present.

One of the obviously strange things Dennis did was to grossly overwork. He claimed that he was trying to establish his value to the family by being helpful. Although his lack of coordination was a problem, he was quite competent in many ways, and he would offer to help or independently take on projects without any rational consideration of what he could accomplish.

One snowy evening shortly after we moved to Fredericksburg, Moe and I came home from work to discover that Dennis was trying to shovel out the entire driveway single-handed. The driveway was the length of a city block, and by this time the snow was about thirty inches deep. When we drove in, he was shoveling at a frantic rate, and had, indeed, been successful in clearing an amazing amount of snow. However, his face was white and he staggered when he walked.

When we sent him into the house he argued bitterly with our attempts to define the job he had undertaken as unrealistic. Finally I gave up and sent him in to take a shower.

Later in the evening, while we had guests, Tom came in, absolutely furious. "Mom! Will you come look at our bathroom!" I followed him to the bathroom the boys shared.

The room was plastered with vomit and feces. Water was splashed around, the walls were smeared, and the mess was unbelievable. I called Dennis.

He came innocently, looked at the mess, and his face drained of color. "I got sick," he faltered.

"That doesn't explain the mess," I told him.

He just looked at me, obviously terrified. "Dennis, you have to say something," I told him. "How do you explain a mess like this?"

"I don't know," he said. "I must have done it. I don't remember!"

I stood helplessly for a moment, trying to think of what to do.

"I'll clean it up," Dennis said.

I thought of all the work in the yard. Making the mess, I knew, was hostile, a baby way of expressing anger, and the anger was related to Dennis's trying to shovel the driveway. It was clearly some kind of pathological game, but there was no way I could pull it together and make sense of it.

I thought of times when my natural children had smeared their cribs and the walls. When they did that they were under a year old. Somewhere in Dennis was a very young Child, angry that he wasn't being taken care of. In spite of all we were doing, it wasn't enough.

"No," I said. "I'll clean it up. If you're still feeling sick, you had better get to bed."

Dennis stood looking at me for a moment, and his eyes filled with tears. "You aren't mad at me?"

"If you hadn't overworked, you wouldn't have been sick," I told him. "I'm not mad about the mess, but I don't like your doing crazy things. After this I want you to check with me before you undertake jobs you haven't been given."

After that incident we supervised everything he did to keep him from overexerting himself. But he kept insisting that he had to prove his worth to us by working, and that we were wrong to try to stop him.

The family structure which we provided for Dennis actually differed little from the structure we already offered Tom and Rickey. We both believe that children grow up to be healthy if they live in a healthy environment. We define home to our children as a place in which we share, love, trust, work and play. A place where problems get solved and feelings are dealt with. The children are encouraged to talk about their feelings and if they have a problem we expect them to be able to tell us openly about it. We are very careful never to lie to the children and we make it clear that all members of the family are expected to be honest and open with one another. Any time someone says, "What are you thinking?" he can expect a straight answer. There are no secrets. Everyone shares responsibility for knowing and caring about what goes on with the other members of the family.

When Moe and I married I converted to Judaism and our household is a Jewish household, an expectation which we communicate to all our children. In all areas of ethical and moral behavior we try to present a clear, consistent image and an even balance of authority and understanding, so that the child is presented with well-defined expectations that are consistently enforced.

It is an essential part of the therapy for the sick children that the mother's and father's roles in the household are clear cut and sharply defined. When a child is newly regressed he needs, more than anything else, a mother's care and attention. He needs to be held and stroked, bathed and fed. Although he is a baby, there are important things that his mother can begin telling him;

"You are a boy—a beautiful boy."

"You aren't bad. You're a good baby."

"Forget all those ugly things. You're my child now. Forget everything but what I tell you."

The messages must be simple because a baby doesn't understand much. He does know if the messages are right for him and make him feel better. He still needs to be protected from the crazy Parent in his head telling him things that make him feel sick and uncomfortable. The child experiences some conflict when the crazy voice escalates the bad messages, but he does not intend to relinquish the mother for things that he knows are unhealthy. So he decides to get rid of the crazy Parent.

The child must be cared for, and kept clean. He cannot be allowed to hurt himself or others. Habit-training is an essential part of growing up, and can begin when the child is still very young.

The father is bigger and stronger and louder than the mother. He makes demands on her which sometimes take precedence over the child's, and he makes decisions which affect the child. He and the mother have a sexual relationship which is mysterious and overwhelming.

It is the father who goes out into the world, and then comes home and tells the children what kind of a place it is. He tells them what to do and how to do it. He shares his masculinity with his sons, telling them what is expected of men and what kind of men they must be. The father is also the object of his daughter's earliest sexual feeling and he helps her know that it is gratifying to be a girl.

As children develop they must be disciplined. We feel that punishment is necessary and should be purposeful, directed at correcting a specific behavior. When a child lies, steals, runs away or mistreats another person, he is promptly punished. Then we assume that is the end of it and that he will not do it again. The child must never be defined as "not all right" or made to feel guilty.

In professional groups the question of using

spanking as a punishment either with regressed babies or with normal children often arises. We have used spanking continuously throughout our experience with rearing both kinds of children and think we have learned a good deal about the effective (as well as the ineffective) use of corporal punishment.

Spanking is effective because while the child is experiencing pain he is unable to discount or otherwise defend himself against the impact of what is being said to him. Consequently, a simple, direct command, such as, "You are not to steal," can be forcibly and permanently imprinted or incorporated by the child entirely against his will, while he is experiencing the spanking.

The mistake many parents make in spanking a child is that they see the purpose of the spanking as retaliating against the child (i.e., punishing him) for the misdeed, or as a way in which they can express anger. The parent who insults the child with name-calling or makes predictions about his future, can expect that the child will incorporate these messages also. I have seen many patients who, while being spanked, were given messages such as, "Why can't you be like other children?" "I can't stand a liar!" "It's ugly and mean to do things like that!" "Shame on you!" etc. All of these were incorporated into the child's head as definitions of himself. Even more damaging are "Do you want to grow up to be a thief and go to jail?" "If you keep that up you'll be nothing but a bum!"

Another frequent mistake parents make when spanking is that they spank a child, but demonstrate no serious expectation that the spanking will be effective in correcting the child's behavior. This expectation is also communicated to the child, who then perceives his behavior as hopelessly bad, beyond the realm of parental control, and who is automatically, as a result of what was said to him during the spanking while he was completely vulnerable, programed to continue the behavior.

A spanking is appropriately conducted briefly and thoroughly, without a great deal of discussion and hand-wringing. The child should be restrained effectively enough that the parent does not have to engage in a physical struggle with him. It should be sufficiently painful that the child cannot defend himself against the pain, and the parent should be sure the child has heard and understood the injunction, i.e., the child should promise not to repeat the behavior. Not, "I'll be good," but "I won't steal," so the spanking is clearly attached to the specific behavior and not related to all the child's behavior or to his character in general.

I was really frightened at the idea of spanking Dennis. Although he functioned most of the time as a very young child, I was quite aware that somewhere tremendous paranoid rage was available, and it seemed most likely to happen if he felt physically threatened. On the other hand, it was very obvious that Dennis would persistently misbehave until I did something about it.

One day when Moe was not at home, a friend came to visit. From the moment the guest walked in the door, it was apparent Dennis did not like him.

When he saw my guest eyeing him a bit warily, Dennis deliberately set out to frighten him. He crawled around the room on all fours, knocking into furniture, dragging things off tables, and even managed to "accidentally" bump my guest. He also did his crazy "puffing up" look and jabbery baby-talk—the perfect impersonation of a big crazy baby.

It was obvious that Dennis was misbehaving and equally obvious that something must be done to stop him—at once. I knew I had to punish him or I would have no control over his behavior at all. Recalling Moe's success with the incident about the clean clothes, I took him into my room and told him how displeased I was with his behavior.

He immediately became very scared; he began to shake and look crazy. It was impossible to tell whether what he was doing was manipulative or if he was really that frightened. I said that I was going to spank him, and although he reacted very fearfully, I had a distinct impression that he was pleased.

Once I had committed myself, I had to go ahead. Dennis did not resist when I pulled him face down on the bed. I whacked him several times with a hairbrush, hard enough so there was no doubt it was hurting him. "You are as responsible for guests as anyone else in this family," I told him. "You aren't ever to misbehave with company again!"

Dennis cried out and shrank away from the

blows. When I stopped he slid down to the floor and sat for a moment with a strange, confused expression. Then his mouth began to tremble, and his lower lip protruded.

"You don't love me!" my great, bearded baby declared. "If you loved me, you wouldn't want to hurt me!"

"If you misbehave, I'm going to punish you, I told you. That's part of what parents do."

"You do love me?" he wanted to know. And, after I had reassured him, he solemnly promised that he would never misbehave with guests again.

I sat back relieved, convinced of the reality of the relationship I was developing with my over-sized son and reassured that I could confidently be his mother in all the ways he needed.

It was not long after that that I had my first confrontation with Dennis's pathology. Paranoia is always related to problems of sexual identity and Dennis had always avoided any direct discussion of sex with me. One evening I had Dennis alone with me in the Laundromat, and, in response to a remark he made I casually referred to a man we both knew, as a homosexual.

There was tense, startled moment. Then, as I watched, Dennis's face changed into the paranoid mask which I was later to know so well. His body seemed to swell. Deep lines cut into his youthful face. His eyes became wild and crazy. He stood snarling over me for a terrifying instant, and then turned and ran out of the Laundromat.

Alarmed, I followed him into the street. But

he had disappeared. I went back inside, puzzled and scared, wondering how long he would remain in the paranoid state and whether he would get into trouble. I wondered if I should contact the police, and realized even as the thought occurred to me that until he did something wrong there was no way they could hold him.

I telephoned Moe, who advised me to do nothing until I got home and we talked it over. He suggested that Dennis might come home himself, when he recovered from the upset. I was also concerned about the possibility that Dennis's anger might evaporate and he would be a frightened three-year-old out alone on a cold and wintry night without even a coat.

When I finished my laundry and left the shopping center, I was relieved to see Dennis walking up the highway toward the Laundromat. I stopped the car and quietly told him to get in. He was obviously still angry, but no longer irrational. I tried to explain to him what I had meant by my remark, and he collapsed crying, in my arms. "I thought I might bite your neck," he told me. "I could feel my face changing and I thought I would turn into a wolf and bite your neck!"

At bedtime Dennis begged for reassurance that he would not turn into a wolf in the night, pleaded with us to allow him to sleep in our room, and when we refused finally dragged his mattress to the floor outside our bedroom and persuaded us to leave the door open so he could call us.

Moe and I lay awake a long time that night, pondering what we should do. Moe was afraid that Dennis would hurt me or the boys. I realized, after the incident at the Laundromat, what I had known all along—that any time the pathology got triggered in Dennis there was no way I could control what he might do.

Moe was especially concerned about an eruption of pathological behavior on Dennis's part at this time. We had not yet moved from Charlottesville to Fredericksburg and, as soon as we found a house, I expected to go ahead alone with the children and get settled while Moe stayed to clear up the details of our leaving Charlottesville.

I had already been working part-time in Fredericksburg, and Moe's transfer to the community Mental Health Clinic there had recently been approved. We were enthusiastic about the move since it would put us closer to the cultural and professional resources of Washington, D.C., and we were both excited at the prospect of working with Don Reed, the dynamic young psychiatrist who was the director of the Mental Health Clinic in Fredericksburg, whom we had both known at the university.

We were concerned, however, about how Dennis might affect our reception there. Fredericksburg is a small (13,000), pretty, historic old town populated primarily by middle-class people. In those days a bearded youth inevitably excited interest and his unusual behavior would surely attract attention. Despite some progress,

Dennis neither looked nor behaved like a normal nineteen-year-old boy.

Then, a few nights later, our family life became even more complicated. We had just returned from a party, around two A.M., and were preparing for bed, when there was an insistent knock at our front door.

There, a strange trio awaited us. A small, sobbing girl, whom Moe and I both recognized at once, clung to the doorsill. Behind her hovered a big, homely, pasty-faced, expressionless boy. At her side, a small Mexican man greeted us apologetically in broken English, then tried to explain what had happened.

"She woke up screaming and screaming. We can't do anything with her."

The tiny, dark-haired girl fell, sobbing hysterically, into Moe's arms. We looked at each other across her dark head and nodded in resignation.

It was obvious that Vickie had also come to our house to stay.

Chapter Four

I HAD KNOWN VICKIE for about two years. When we first moved to Charlottesville I saw her at a Friends Meeting with her father and brother, and was interested in the withdrawn little Mexican-Jewish girl because she was so obviously seriously disturbed and seemed to be getting very little help.

When I heard that Vickie had regressed and was hospitalized I took her a doll, knowing that there would be no support for her regressive needs from anyone on the hospital staff. However, she was unresponsive to me and I did not visit her again.

John, her pale-faced younger brother, I got to know a little better; not that it was easy to get to know John. He was a silent, sullen-looking boy, who sometimes served as a volunteer in the children's hospital where I had worked.

Later I learned that Vickie did not do well in the University hospital and was eventually transferred to a state hospital. It was there that Moe met her and took an interest in her, not knowing of my previous contacts. I was pleased when I found out that he was seeing her and trying to help her get well enough to leave the hospital.

Unfortunately, when she was discharged from

the hospital, Vickie returned to the same situation which had caused her sickness originally. She was an undifferentiated schizophrenic and her worst problem was the depressed apathy that left her drained of all motivation. In her home Vickie spent most of the day sitting alone, living in a fantasy world, relating to no one (her mother had died when Vickie was thirteen, her father worked, and John had gone away to college).

The night she came to our house she had been awakened during the night when her brother, who was home for the weekend, came into her bedroom to borrow her alarm clock. She began to scream and could not be consoled. She begged to be brought to our house, and her father and brother had helplessly complied.

While Moe took Vickie into the office to try to find out what was happening, I offered her father and brother some coffee. Her father spoke sadly of his inability to care for Vickie and said he had decided that she would have to be returned to the hospital. John simply sat, his face blank. I tried to find out if he felt responsible for upsetting her, but my questions seemed only to confuse him.

I finally gave up trying to talk to them and went to the office where Moe was attempting to comfort the sobbing girl. "I can't send her away like this," he said. "Can we put her up for the night?"

Of course we could. Our house was a sprawling, expandable, ranch-style dwelling and while we didn't have a separate bedroom for

Vickie, there was room for her to sleep in the office. I went back to the living room to send John and her father home. They were obviously relieved that we were taking charge, and I promised to be in touch with them the next day.

When we were alone in the living room I stopped to reassure Dennis for a minute. He had waited up for us, and since Vickie had arrived he had been looking very young and scared. Now he clung to me. "Is she going to the hospital?" he wanted to know. "What's going to happen to her?"

"I don't know, Dennis," I said. "You stay in here."

Back in the office with Moe and Vickie, I found that she had quieted. But when I sat down beside her, she drew away from me. "Are you going to be my mother?" she asked. She stiffened when I reached out to stroke her cheek, and then relaxed, and let me take her into my arms.

"I wonder what Dennis will think," Moe said.

"I guess you'd better call him," I suggested.

Dennis came into the room looking very young and uncoordinated. He stared at Vickie in my arms for a moment, struggled helplessly for words, and then stumbled toward her, making infantile noises. She cried out in fright, and he stopped, then sat on the floor and tried to talk to her, and to us. He didn't want us to send her to the hospital; she could not get well there. He wanted her to stay with us. They would get well together.

Now we had two schizophrenic babies.

Vickie was much harder to care for than Dennis. Her thinking was disconnected and confused and if she were left alone she might sit passively for hours. At other times she did unexpected crazy things, like running outdoors barefoot in the snow. She had to be supervised constantly.

By the second day Dennis was obviously jealous of his new little sister, and went around looking alternately angry and depressed. Since his mother had stopped caring for him when his own little sister was born, it was easy to understand what was happening to him. But when I tried to talk about his feelings, he would simply walk away.

When I went in to put Dennis to bed that night he appeared to have been crying. For the first time he reached his arms out to me.

"What's the matter, little boy?" I asked him.

"I didn't think you'd come any more."

"Of course I will," I promised.

"No you won't," he wept. "You'll have to send me away."

"Why, Dennis?"

"Because I'll hurt her."

I called Moe, and together we reassured Dennis, telling him that we could protect Vickie, that he was just as important to us as she was, and that we loved them both. He rather dubiously accepted the comfort. After that he alternately expressed jealousy and protectiveness toward Vickie.

Vickie was a handful in many ways. We had her with us one day when we were house hunting in Fredericksburg. Moe had gone into an office with the real estate agent and I was alone in the car in a parking lot with Vickie when she, for no apparent reason, began to act up.

"I'm scared," she whimpered.

"There's nothing to be scared of," I told her. "Stop that, Vickie!" I honked the car horn, signaling Moe to come back, knowing that Vickie was going to start screaming any moment.

I anticipated the first screech by just a moment, yanked Vickie face down across my lap, and spanked her soundly. When Moe and the real estate agent came out to the car, Vickie was weeping like any little girl who had been paddled, and since she looked about twelve years old (she was actually twenty-two) the realtor didn't react with much surprise.

Before we got away from Fredericksburg Vickie did start screaming, and we had to take her to the hospital where she could be sedated. The staff at the Fredericksburg hospital were very friendly and understanding, and I was pleased that our new community had such a good emergency service. I didn't realize then how familiar the emergency room at the hospital would soon become.

On the way home Moe and I talked seriously, while Vickie slept, drugged, in the back seat, about whether we had taken on too much. Supervising Vickie seemed beyond our resources, especially since she didn't sleep at all well, and I was with her day and night. Moe pointed out that I was exhausted, and that it wasn't fair to Dennis or the little boys.

Part of the problem was that Vickie was not

newly regressed. She did not relate to us as a baby in the same way Dennis did, and I did not feel as confident in mothering her. Moe had been her therapist before she came to us and she felt close to him, but she was not equally committed to letting me be her mother.

The relationship was hard for me, too, because of emotional conflicts of my own. My first natural child, a dark-skinned little girl with curly black hair, had died in infancy. Her name was Vikki. There were still many feelings around my daughter's death that I was unwilling to deal with, and being presented with a daughter by the same name and same general physical characteristics was activating old fears and guilt. That, added to the fact she was not a baby, kept me from accepting her as my child, in the sense that Dennis was.

The situation with Vickie seemed to grow worse instead of better. It became obvious that her episodes of acting out were ways of controlling me. She was furiously angry with her natural mother, whom she described as cold and uncaring, preferring her brother John to her; she was bitter about her mother's death, obviously perceiving that as the ultimate rejection. I could not tell whether she was punishing me for the things her mother did (or didn't) do, or whether she actually felt that she needed that much attention in order to be safe.

One afternoon when she and I were in the basement, she got angry at me. We started to walk up the stairs when she turned unexpectedly and pitched herself head-first downward.

She landed dazed and bruised, but essentially unhurt, and when I asked why she had done it, she laughed and said it was because she was mad at me.

Moe was furious. "We've had enough!" he told me. He contacted Vickie's father, and together they took her to the hospital. When he found she'd gone, Dennis was inconsolable.

During the next few days I became seriously concerned about Dennis. I knew he was angry and frightened about our "giving up"; that it threatened his security with us. He insisted he didn't blame us, that he understood what we had done, but I knew he was speculating that a time would come when we could not handle him.

I also experienced a great deal of grief around the loss of the pretty, dark little girl I had tried to claim as a daughter. For two nights after Vickie left I had nightmares in which I was somehow inadequate as a mother and this resulted in the death of a child. All my nights had been sleepless since Vickie had been with us, and I felt physically and emotionally exhausted. But I got little relief after she was gone.

On the third day Moe telephoned me from the hospital. I knew that some of the medical staff were trying to persuade Moe that we should make another try with Vickie, suggesting that medication could be used to control her acting up, but Moe, having made the decision that we could not care for her, was reluctant to reconsider. However, now he was excited. "I'd like you to come over to the hospital and talk to Vickie," he said. "She seems to have worked something out and she sounds completely different!"

At the hospital I found that Vickie was indeed different. She was no longer confused and incoherent. Instead, she greeted me purposefully and said that she was eager to tell me something.

What she told me was that she had two personalities. Her name, she said, was not Vickie at all. It was Rosita, the Mexican name given her by her father. When she was about eleven years old, and she and John and her mother had moved to Charlottesville from New York City, she had changed her name to Vickie, and refused to answer to any other name. Her mother, who had separated from her husband and did not like the Mexican name anyway, was willing for her to do that, and it had seemed a simple thing.

Inside her head, however, it was not so simple. Along with giving up the name, she had tried to deny all of the characteristics she associated with the little New York Jewish-Mexican girl. Rosita she perceived as stupid, scared, unable to do things. Vickie was going to be sexy, grand, and successful.

Much of the pathology we had seen in Vickie was a result of her shifting back and forth from the Vickie to the Rosita personalities. Since neither personality had a full range of affect (for example, Vickie expressed anger, Rosita could not; Rosita experienced fear and pain, Vickie could not), whenever an experience occurred which was not consistent with one she would switch to the other. Since the two personalities did not share memories, much of her confusion occurred because of these shifts.

Rosita was not sure exactly what should be done about the problem. She knew that Vickie was unreal, and suggested that probably Rosita, despicable as she was, was the true Natural Child, and should be reinforced. She should no longer be called Vickie and would have to give up the advantages available to her in that bolder, more resourceful self (which we later came to call her Adapted Child).

It was obvious to me that the two personalities would have to be integrated, since neither was completely independent of the other. Rosita agreed that it would be possible to do that and that she was willing to try.

So we took her home from the hospital.

Shortly after that the children and I moved to Fredericksburg, in the middle of one of the worst snow-storms ever to hit Virginia. The move was unbelievably chaotic. It was freezing cold and it took a full day before we could get the house heated properly. We huddled before a fire in the fireplace, trying to figure out what we could burn for warmth, or closed ourselves in the kitchen which we could heat with the oven. We could not get our car up the driveway, and in the process of moving and packing, none of the supplies we needed to cope with the weather were available. The children were all irritable and indignant that I was not taking better care of them. It seemed to them that I wasn't managing things well at all. Dennis was afraid of the moving men, and Rosita complained bitterly that he was "acting like an ass," and embarrassing her. Finally a Fredericksburg friend with a pickup truck rescued us, getting an adequate supply of groceries up the driveway, and we began to get acquainted with our new home, where we still live.

It is a large, single level house spread across the top of a hill, at the edge of Battlefield Park. There are Civil War trenches in our back yard. We have a generous yard around the house and approximately two acres of wooded land for the children to play in. At the time we moved in, the house consisted of three large bedrooms, a small family room, an enormous living and dining room, and a sun porch. As time passed, the living room got changed into a combination dining-playroom, and the smaller dining area was used for sitting space. The porch was divided into two bedrooms, and the large garage into a boys' dormitory. Both the house and the grounds around it have proved amazingly comfortable and adequate to accommodate our growing family.

At the time we moved in, we did not expect our family to grow. We were involved enough in solving problems with our two new members, in addition to getting Tom and Rickey settled in their new home. We expected Chuck, my oldest natural son who was in San Francisco with his father, to return to us that summer, and anticipated that five would make up our family.

During this period, following her return from the hospital, Rosita seemed to be getting along very well. She was working at integrating her two selves, and was pleased at her successes. We began to talk to her about taking a course at Mary Washington College during the spring semester and she was scared but pleased at our confidence that she could do that.

We were surprised at how well the children got along together. Dennis and Rosita were very interested in helping one another work out problems, and Tom and Rosita got to be very close. Tom related to Dennis as an older brother to a baby, but he became actively involved in caring for Rosita. He held and stroked her when she needed reassurance, and in spite of being twelve years older chronologically, Rosita accepted his parenting. One afternoon when I came in from a short errand, I found Tom sitting in a rocking chair, holding Rosita on his lap, rocking and comforting her. Dennis, Tom explained to me, had scared Rosita and Tom had told him to go sit in a chair and behave himself while he comforted the frightened girl.

For all his apparent lackadaisical manner, Tom had a way of absorbing information and picking up clues without appearing to be aware of what was going on. Occasionally his knowledge and sophistication startled me. Rosita had a curious habit of twitching, in a series of violent jerks that involved her entire body, starting with her head. I had asked her several times about this, but she never gave me a straight answer. One evening, when we were all sitting around the living room, I watched Rosita's violent jerking for a few moments and then said, "I wonder what it is that she's doing?"

"She's masturbating," calmly observed ten-year-old Tom, and went back to his comic book.

Rosita threw Tom a startled, angry look, then sat very still. It was the last time we saw her twitch.

I guess Tom must have been right. But I didn't know that he even knew the word.

Tom was worried that Dennis might hurt Rickey. We never saw him do anything threatening, but on several occasions Tom was certain Dennis's reactions to Rickey were not innocent little-boy playfulness. One time the boys accidently woke Dennis early one morning, and Tom reported that Dennis had "looked real crazy" and threatened Rickey with his fist. Dennis denied that anything had really happened, and it was difficult to tell whether the boys were over-reacting because they were frightened of Dennis's size, or if he had deliberately tried to frighten them.

Some schizophrenics experience a chronological regression where they grow from infancy through adolescence, experiencing only one stage at a time. Dennis, however, varied from one age to another. When he first regressed in my arms, he seemed clearly a young infant, but after that he usually appeared to be about three years old, with episodes of oral and anal behavior, such as drooling and temper outbursts. We did not yet know enough about regression to know how much of his childhood Dennis needed to re-experience or how long each phase would take.

There was so much we didn't know. It was difficult to distinguish pathology from regressive needs and we guessed at which behavior to support and which to discourage. Much of the time we simply reacted on the basis of how we would have reacted to a normal child if he had behaved as Dennis did, but that was difficult, too, because of his size and the maturity of his thinking. Dennis, probably not understanding the depth of our puzzlement, put an enormous (and perhaps costly) effort into answering our questions.

He related to me much better than he did to Moe, whom he obviously perceived as a potentially powerful and dangerous enemy who must be placated and tolerated, but avoided as much as possible. He asked for frequent reassurances that Moe was not going to separate him from me, and sometimes he needed permission or encouragement from Moe to work out a particular problem, but much of the time he reacted fearfully or with sullen politeness when Moe was around.

As Dennis's second month with us came to an end, a decision had to be made as to whether or not he should return to the University for the spring semester. We were reluctant to agree to his going, but hesitant about insisting that he stay with us when he believed he could function at school. He was clearly in better condition than when he came to us, and there were friends in Charlottesville who could help look after him.

We would know, now, that it is a mistake to expect a child as sick as Dennis was to live a grown-up life away from home, and later Dennis was to express bitterness about our letting him do it. However, we agreed that he could return to his apartment, which had been maintained in Charlottesville, and that we would support him psychologically with frequent phone calls and drop-in visits. He planned to come home each weekend and agreed to return any time during the week he felt seriously upset.

Actually, Dennis spent at least half of the semester at home, usually attending classes Monday and Tuesday and then coming home for a couple of days, returning for Friday classes, and coming back for the weekend. In spite of his frequent absences, he did better in his school-work that semester than he had done since he entered college.

Because of our concern over Dennis's being on his own so much, we began to press him to work out the psychosis when he was at home. This, too, we have since realized was a mistake. It is not really necessary to push a sick child to get well in most instances; certainly not with any-one as motivated as Dennis always was. If the youngster is sick enough, he can hardly avoid having psychotic episodes, and the main problem is to teach him to send out signals so that a safe situation can be set up for working them through. While we were encouraging Dennis to work through problems, we were not, at that time, aware of how to provide a structure in which he could feel assured no one could be hurt.

In opening up a psychosis and attempting to resolve it, the child cannot be held responsible for his behavior. In many instances he does not know what is going to happen until he gets into the episode. We later learned to set up a group situation which provides maximum protection for everyone involved. The child tells us that he has something to work out, and a group of ten to twenty people gathers, making sure that there are enough strong boys to control anything which can possibly happen (including satellite upsets by others present). All furniture and possible weapons are cleared away, and the child is placed in the middle of the circle. The child is then told to "do what you need to do," and until he presents an actual threat to himself or to other people, he is allowed to get completely into the psychosis.

After an episode of acting out a psychosis, the child is usually physically and emotionally exhausted, and this is a time when we engage in what we call "scripting." Whatever confusion and misperceptions have been revealed during the psychotic episode are carefully corrected through parental definition. For example, many children show confusion about the differences between thinking, feeling and acting. "It is not possible for one person to get inside another person," we tell them. "Every person is completely separate from every other person. Each of us thinks and feels things which other people cannot know about unless we tell them. People relate and communicate to one another through the way they behave, not with what they think or feel."

While the patient is fully activated to his Child state—dependent and vulnerable—the "scripting" has much more impact than at other times.

Although we did a lot of scripting with Dennis, we were not prepared to restrain him or provide "protection" while he worked out psychoses. Yet we often demanded that he work out problems, without being aware of the dangers which might result if he attempted to do so. He responded to these demands with evasions and negativism, and a pattern of passive-aggressive behavior (where anger is expressed through a refusal to act) began to be established. Our inability to provide the structure Dennis needed to work through problems meant, in some instances, that the psychosis erupted unexpectedly in violent episodes.

When Dennis did work through problems, he told us afterward that his Adult seemed to be standing on the sidelines observing what was going on.

My voice is coming to me from a great distance. I can hear it, but it is disembodied, floating above my head. I am here writhing on the floor, but I am also there, where my voice is, watching myself, analyzing what I am doing. . . .

We learned a great deal from Dennis. One of the things, which was to prove true of all the other schizophrenic children, was that he incorporated the messages we gave him literally, word for word. When Dennis was older and had been temporarily left in charge of the household, he caught one of the girls raiding the refrigerator for ice cream, and he smacked her so hard she fell across the room, frightening her and the other children. One of our house rules is that the children are not permitted to slap or strike one another, and when Moe disciplined Dennis for having hit the girl, he said angrily, "Don't you ever lay a hand on your sister again."

A day or so later, when Dennis's assistance was needed in restraining the same girl, he found himself absolutely unable to touch her. He had incorporated the parental message as a specific prohibition against touching her with his hands. Before he was able to touch her, Moe had to replace the "don't touch" message with "don't hit. . . ."

Another thing we discovered is that the schizophrenic youngster is what we have come to call "scriptbound." Most of us are able to rebel against or otherwise disobey parental messages if we choose, but schizophrenics, at least while they are very sick and during the early period of treatment, cannot. Thus, there was literally no way Dennis could have "touched" his sister under the circumstances without becoming acutely upset himself.

Dennis had been back in Charlottesville attending school for several weeks and appeared to have passed through infancy and early childhood, seeming to be in about mid-latency (maybe ten years old) when one Saturday morning, for no apparent reason, he got down on the floor and began crawling around like a baby under two.

Moe and I stared at him in dismay. He had apparently graduated from that stage several weeks earlier, and we assumed that once a child progressed to another, older, age level, he should not slip back to an earlier period.

"What is it, Dennis?" we asked. "What are you doing?"

He peered up with the owlish squint of a crawling baby, and said nothing. Then he lost interest in us, rolled over on his back, pulled his belt loose from his trousers and began dangling the metal buckle of his belt in front of his eyes, as though it were a rattle.

"Dennis, answer me!" I demanded.

He peered up at me again, as though I were ten feet tall, and silently shook his head from side to side.

As Dennis made gurgling baby noises Moe and I looked at each other helplessly. We were both frightened. We knew that previous attempts at supporting regression had resulted in the patients' becoming fixated in the regression and not motivated to grow up. Did this mean that Dennis had re-regressed back to pre-verbal infancy? Had he somehow lost his functional Adult? Or was he possibly just being perverse, wanting to frighten us in retaliation for the pressure we had been putting on him to resolve problems?

He was much more energetic and demanding than he had been previously when acting a very young child. This time he moved around vigorously, knocking things over, pulling things down, and crying loudly when we interfered. It did not occur to us that his behavior was more typical of a crawling baby now than it had been before.

When we found him in the same condition on the following day, Moe and I panicked. For some reason we were both convinced that it was extremely important to keep Dennis functional so he could go to school. It did not occur to either of us that he might be doing something necessary to his getting well, or that he might be trying to work something out on an infantile level where he was manageable, something that might have been beyond our resources had he tried to work it out as a ten-year-old.

We decided that what he was doing was crazy and unnecessary, and that we would have to make him stop it. We confronted him angrily with the demand that he become functional again or we would refuse to take care of him.

After an hour or so, when he realized that we were determined, Dennis did stop. He got off the floor and acted Adult, but seemed confused and distressed, unwilling to talk about what had happened. We were very relieved to get him back to functioning, and didn't demand much explanation, assuming that he was playing some kind of game and was now ashamed of what he had done. We gave him clear messages that we expected him to behave as maturely and responsibly as was possible for him and that we would not permit any lingering in the regression.

What we did in that instance is exactly what happens to regressed patients in more conventional treatment settings. Later on, when Dennis was more functional, we were confronted with unresolved problems from infancy at a time when working them out was seriously disruptive to him. Our error was that we did not trust our huge infant's powerful urge for survival.

Beginning with Dennis, but also from the other children, we have learned to have a great deal of confidence in how much the children know about themselves. Most schizophrenic children know they need parenting to get well and beg for it. They often have a fantasy of what good parenting and a healthy family life would be like. Desperately many of them try to get parenting from therapists or other parent figures. One of our children tells of pleading with her woman therapist, "Touch me, hold me, reassure me," and the doctor drew back, saying, "Yes, I understand that you need that, but I'm not prepared to help you that way."

Few professionals are willing to risk intimacy with a patient. Part of this is their training. But another part is an apparently common repugnance to any form of intimacy with people outside of one's immediate family. I once attended a life-saving class during which there was an exhibition of mouth-to-mouth resuscitation, and the mother next to me commented, "I could do that to my own child, but not to a stranger." Several others present agreed. Even though the alternative might be death.

Intimacy, love, are the keys to a sick child's recovery, infinitely more powerful than medication and theory. Overwhelmed with unmet needs, the child must have the feel of love.

Love was something Moe and I could easily offer. It was more difficult, though, to learn to accept responsibility for the mistakes as well as the successes. Our investment in the children cost us a great deal of anguish when our errors or lack of knowledge become apparent in failures with the children. We have never been entirely successful in defining the errors as inevitable and excusable in the overall framework of what we were trying to do.

We had only been settled in Fredericksburg for a few weeks when we acquired yet another child, Rosita's white-faced brother, John. The tall, quiet boy had become a familiar visitor, but remained essentially unknown to us, since it was nearly impossible to engage him in any kind of conversation.

We had heard that John was about to be jailed for draft evasion. I knew that John was a dedicated pacifist, very sincere in his religious beliefs. I did not doubt that his failure to report for induction was a deliberate act of civil disobedience on his part, but it seemed to me ridiculous that a youngster who was clearly too emotionally disturbed to be inducted into military service should be sent to jail.

Moe and I talked it over, and decided that since John had never discussed the matter with us, it was not our business to interfere. However, our patients in Charlottesville thought differently. "You aren't going to let them send John to jail?" they demanded indignantly.

Finally I agreed to speak to John about it. The next time he visited us, only a few days before the hearing at which he was to be sentenced, I said to him, "John, I think it's pretty silly for you to go to jail!"

To my amazement, he started to cry, and for the first time John talked to me, trying to explain the confusion he was experiencing, his fear of violence, the ethics and principles that were part of his religious conviction and his assurance that he could not survive either military life or jail. I had not known about his problems in college or his inability to compete for and hold a job, nor had I known that he had had previous contacts with psychotherapists.

It took some frantic maneuvering, and the cooperation of attorneys, courts, and military authorities, before the whole thing was straightened out, but when John went to court the charges were dropped on the basis of the psychiatric problem, and a few days later John joined our family.

John was very different from Rosita and Dennis. He found it difficult to talk to any of us, and for a long time his needs were communicated through a kind of mute dependency. For instance, John would never show that he wanted attention. Instead he would stand around in doorways which I might eventually need to pass through. I quickly learned that finding John blocking my path was a sign that he needed attention, and I learned to offer him a quick hug whenever I stumbled into him.

I also learned very quickly why John was so pale and gaunt. He had one of the worst eating problems I have ever seen. Eating, he explained to me, was a bad habit, and should be avoided whenever possible. When I tried to explain nutrition, he discounted whatever I said: "You can't know that that stuff applies to me. Maybe people are different. It isn't reasonable to say everyone's the same." Eventually I gave up efforts at explanation and simply demanded that John eat what I considered to be good for him.

John was eager to please us and be helpful, and was more able to do things than Rosita or Dennis, and I tried to think of things to keep him busy. When he had been with us only a week or so, I asked him to paint a wall dividing two rooms. Looking at the wall, I said, "Have you ever used spray paint?" He said he had not, and I said, "Well, instead of buying brushes and stuff it might be simpler to do it that way."

John dropped me off at work and I gave him ten dollars to buy a couple of cans of spray paint.

When he picked me up that evening, I knew at once that John was extremely upset. He was trembling and refusing to look at me. I asked what was the matter, but he interrupted me to demand, "What kind of paint did you ask me to get?"

What had happened, I discovered, was that John had bought a couple of cans of spray paint and started on the wall. The paint covered only a small area. He had spent the remainder of the ten dollars on more cans of paint, convinced that he must be doing something wrong. When that didn't finish the job either, he then spent all of his own pocket money on more paint. Still only half the wall was covered.

Convinced that I would blame him for not succeeding, he first asked what paint I had told him to get. He was afraid that if I knew the paint had not worked I would say I had given him different instructions. Apparently John's experience with parents was that if things went wrong, it was always his fault, and he was protecting himself from my lying.

When John first came to us, it was clear that he believed all his Child needs to be selfish and wrong. Eating, sleeping, playing, were not permissible to the Parent inside John's head. However, John's Child so strongly desired a car of his own that he overcame the denial of his Parent. It was this desire which eventually motivated John to find and hold a job, and sometimes I think John's red Karmann Ghia had as much to do with his getting well as we did.

Dennis did not seem to be jealous of John at all, the way he had been of Rosita; and the two boys became, and continue to be, very close, although they are so different. Rosita, however, was very afraid of my favoring John over her, as she believed her natural mother to have done. Actually, I think their mother, whom we know to have been very sick, was unable to do much for either of the children. Although their disturbances were different in many ways, the two children shared problems having to do with not being able to express their feelings. They had grown up together in a household where apparently there was very little communication.

John could not identify feeling angry, nor could he in any way express anger. Sometimes when he was upset and shaking I knew he was mad about something specific, but it was a long time before he was able to get in touch with those feelings.

Anger, however, began to be a serious problem with Dennis.

On one occasion, when we were all sitting at the dinner table, Dennis and I were arguing. He was insisting that an IQ of 140 was "stupid" and I was maintaining that it certainly was not. Dennis, unexpectedly enraged, grabbed a heavy glass and threatened to throw it at me.

Everyone was startled and frightened except Dennis himself, who, after such incidents, always discounted the seriousness of his potential violence.

On a weekend not long after that, when David Rohrer, the young graduate student who originally brought Dennis to us, and was later to work for us, was visiting, we were all outside shoveling snow. Dennis, as usual, was trying to demonstrate how much work he could do, and was indignant when David and John and I began playing.

Dennis yelled something disagreeable to us about not working, and as a reply I ran toward him and tossed a snowball at his chest.

Dennis reacted instantly, swinging the heavy shovel in his hands directly at my head in a powerful blow that might, had it landed, have decapitated me. John and David both jumped at Dennis, grabbing him and intercepting the blow, then we all stood frozen for a moment. Dennis, still looking paranoid, did not resist when I took the shovel out of his hands.

Dennis's paranoid expression, like all paranoid

expressions, was very scary. In trying to describe it, all I can refer to are horror movies remembered from my childhood, insanely laughing madmen plotting against innocent victims. The paranoid looks quite apparently crazy; his body puffs up angrily, his eyes are wide and shining, his face twisted into a sadistic grimace. Often paranoids smile meaninglessly or laugh with macabre glee.

As I was later to learn, what happens in a paranoid episode is fairly simple. The paranoid patient is always feeling fear and anger; because this is so constantly a part of his experience, he does not understand that other people see life differently. He believes the entire world is balanced on the thin edge of violence, and is terrified that at any instant the violence may be directed at him.

When something happens to frighten him, he reacts immediately with anger in an attempt to avoid feeling afraid. He expects that if he does experience the fear he will become immobilized or "frozen" and be unable to react to the problem. Anger, however, has a physiological effect quite opposite to fear. The person feels a flush of energy and strong impulses to react vigorously and aggressively. This results in two serious problems: One is that anger is often not an appropriate substitute for fear; the other is that there is no Adult thinking about the situation, no information about the seriousness of the threat, and the amount of energy (or anger) experienced is unrelated to the cause.

Moe, who had been working some distance

from us, came running up to us, trembling from fright.

"If you ever do that again, we'll put you in a hospital!" he yelled at Dennis. "You promise me you'll never threaten her again—or get out of here right now!"

Dennis stared at him silently, then marched into the house. Moe and I followed him. He had gone to our room and was lying across the bed, face down. We tried to talk to him. At first he was defiant. He denied swinging the shovel at me, claimed no memory of the whole incident. Moe said that Dennis had better remember, because we had had enough of his crazy behavior, that we were unwilling to take a chance on his killing anybody.

"Well, why don't you punish me then?" Dennis finally yelled furiously.

Moe took off his belt and whipped him. Dennis did not flinch. His face was set in hard, angry lines.

When Moe had finished, Dennis said, "I didn't feel anything. Maybe you better lock me up."

Disgusted, Moe threw the belt down. "If you don't want to be hospitalized, you'd better do something!" he shouted, and walked out of the room.

When Moe walked out of the room, Dennis suddenly became Child again and clung to me, whimpering.

"Please don't give me up, Mommy," he begged. "Please don't." He went on to explain that he could not tell me how he was really feeling in front of Moe because Moe was so angry. He talked, rationally, about his fear of hurting people, about the fact that his own mother had never punished him.

"You punish me!" Dennis said. "It will only mean something if you do it."

I hesitated, both because Moe had already whipped him, and also because I was somehow uncomfortable with what was happening. But I could not determine what was wrong with what he was saying, and it was apparent that something had to be done.

"I think this is a serious matter," I told him. "If I punish you for trying to kill me, it'll be more serious than just a spanking. I'll make sure that you feel it," I promised.

He obviously did not believe that I could.

I picked up the belt and struck him full force.

"You weren't kidding!" he cried out in an adult rational voice.

I struck him five more times. He became very young, doubled up screaming, his fingers in his mouth. "Please, please, Mommy, I'll be good!"

Afterward he cried very hard for a long time, saying over and over, "I'll never hit anybody again. My mommy doesn't want me to hurt people." He babbled at length about how bad he was, unfit to live with Rosita and me; then, less regressed, he clung to me again. "Maybe that wasn't enough," he said. "Maybe you should punish me more."

I thought he had been punished quite enough. I comforted him, and told him, "It isn't up to you to decide how severe punishment should be." Later I was to find, to my chagrin, that Dennis learned from this that a good way to get comfort and attention from me was to get into trouble, and then act very ashamed and contrite. Although I had no clue at the time, my comforting him was one of the mistakes which set the stage for the passive aggressive game that was to develop between us.

At dinner that night Dennis was flushed and infantile. He played with his food and whispered, in a very gratified way, "Punished. Punished. My mommy really punished me!" He would not look at Moe and whenever Moe addressed him, Dennis looked to me for instructions in how to answer.

After dinner, when Rosita wanted to discuss the afternoon's event with Dennis, he flatly refused to discuss it with her. Until then they had shared everything, and Rosita was indignant about his shutting her out.

It was a bad day in many ways, although it took time to assess all the damage that had been done.

I had difficulty going to sleep that night. Intellectually I had known all along that the schizophrenic children would probably want to kill me.

But this was the first time that I had experienced the fact emotionally.

Chapter Five

In early april, some college students whom I had worked with in group therapy called me to see if I would conduct a group for them if they drove to Fredericksburg.

They arrived, on the appointed afternoon, in one car. The students were all familiar to me except for one girl. She was a slight, beautiful girl of about eighteen with long, straight brown hair, a pale, delicately featured face and saucer-shaped brown eyes. Her name, her friends told me, was Elizabeth. She ignored me and the rest of the group, retired to a corner of the room which I used for an office, and curled into a ball, her shoulders hunched forward and her head lowered so that her hair blanketed her face.

I don't know why I came today. They said she would be able to tell me how sick I am. But I don't believe it. I've been sick so long and nobody helps me. I know I'm getting worse each day and I'm so scared. I lie and I steal and I drink and I hurt people—all the things the Sisters taught me not to do—and it makes me feel wicked. But no one stops me. Yesterday I stole a huge pile of candy and ran down the hall shouting into the other girls' ears, "Let's have a party!" I was going to share the candy, but they all ran away. . . .

Everyone's afraid of me now. The school wants to kick me out but my parents won't let me come home. They don't know what to do with me either. No one does. I'm not me any more. I don't know who I am. I either feel so good I think I'll faint. Or so bad I'm sure I'll die. Either way I always feel like I'm just about to EXPLODE—"

As I looked at the figure huddled in the corner the only thing I knew about this child was that she was obviously very sick, very angry and frightened. I had to find some way to reach out to her. I stood directly over her, called her name and held out my hand.

—Oh, don't make me look at you! Don't try to touch me!

Suddenly I saw a flash and she sprang at me, like a jungle cat, kicking, raining blows with her hard little fists before I could defend myself. The other kids grabbed her and between us we finally got her into a chair with her arms pinioned behind her back and her legs gripped at the ankles.

She continued to rage convulsively for some time while we tried to hold her. She gnashed her teeth and fought with an incredible strength considering her slight size. Eventually her furious screams died into pitiful sobbing, her body went limp, and we were able to relax our grip on her and inspect our wounds.

All of us had been scratched or bruised. I had large, swollen bruises in several places where she had kicked me. I had seen patients out of control before, but I had experienced nothing so completely unexpected as this.

When she had quieted and we could talk to her, Elizabeth seemed bewildered by what we told her, and utterly unable to comprehend what had happened. She recalled being upset and frightened at my approaching her, but she was angry and insisted that she had been only frightened.

She was obviously, as her young friends who had brought her to me had realized, an emergency case. Before I had even spoken with them, I was already furious with her parents for allowing this youngster to be free from supervision.

I telephoned them at once, described what had happened, and told them Elizabeth was urgently in need of residential care. They expressed much concern but there was no evidence that they were interested in responsible plans. "We had so hoped that things could be worked out—" her mother said vaguely. She did, however, agree for us to take her.

When I then told Elizabeth that we wanted her to stay with us, she asked no questions, but accepted with delight, like a little girl invited to visit.

Oh, I'm so glad she'll let me stay. I like it here. It feels so safe and quiet. I hurt her but she's not afraid of me. She shows me love. If I stay, maybe I won't be so frightened all the time. . . .

With the help of her friends, the staff at the college where she had been enrolled, and her parents (who seemed the least informed of all), I pieced together Elizabeth's story. The second of four children in a middle-class family, she had apparently been sick for a number of years. She had a long history of trouble: lying, stealing, drinking, drugs and sexual perversion. She had made several suicide attempts. Yet, during much of this time her parents had assumed that she would outgrow such gross disturbances. She had never been hospitalized, although she had at times been under private treatment. When the first therapist who saw her demanded that the family be involved in the treatment, Elizabeth's mother had been unwilling to participate and therapy was dropped. At fifteen, she left home and entered a convent to become a nun, but the Sisters had not felt that she could make the adjustment to religious life and she was shortly returned home. At a second therapist's suggestion, she again left home and entered college.

At the time I met her, she was living in the college dormitory but not attending classes. She stayed in her room most of the days sleeping.

About twice weekly, when she felt upset, Elizabeth screamed. She had once heard her mother say, "I get so upset I could scream," and on the basis of the parental message she periodically erupted into violent, convulsive shrieks. Generally someone at the college telephoned for an ambulance and she was carted off to an emergency room, sedated and released to her parents who returned her to the college dorm. The college authorities told me that they had asked her parents to remove her from the school since she was obviously too unwell to live independently, but the parents had been ignoring their demands. The college was contemplating taking legal action.

Dennis had been seriously sick when we took him. But Elizabeth was sicker. She had no functional behavior at all. It seemed incredible to me that neither of her parents had faced how tragically ill she was.

When my parents take me to see a doctor, I don't say a word. I just watch while my mother lies to the doctor and my father shakes his head. Once I was screaming and screaming and my father was lying on the bed in my room watching me. When I stopped screaming and lunged at him to get comfort, he didn't make a move to touch me. He drew back, saying, "What you need is a nice summer job!"

Elizabeth was a fairly typical hebephrenic schizophrenic. Hebephrenia is the schizophrenic disturbance with the worst possible prognosis. It is colloquially called "the death sentence" in many hospitals since hebephrenics are traditionally locked up in back wards and forgotten.

They are usually diagnosed rather late because they don't look or act like other schizophrenics. They appear naïve, childlike and are often quite appealing. In the early stages they are adaptable and appear "sweet and good" and conforming. During that phase they are not subject to depression, nor do they withdraw. At times they seem silly and giddy, and are apt to do strange things with words, such as rhyming or garbling them. But as they get sicker they take on a Jekyll and Hyde personality, and their sweet and good behavior is alternated with acts of convulsive violence (which may look like seizures) or periods of blackouts in which they do unacceptable things with no memory of the events.

Hebephrenics can, at will, elevate their moods so they are constantly "high." They giggle. They jiggle. They may appear charged with fathomless energy—or completely inert. When a hebephrenic is being giddy, you can assume he is on the verge of an episode. But the hebephrenic can also go directly into an episode without warning, since the anger is always there, ready to be triggered. Because of this, they pose a constant danger to themselves and to others. Since they are considered virtually untreatable, and present a threat to society or their own safety, they are usually locked up as soon as they are diagnosed. To my knowledge, no one had ever cured a hebephrenic before we took Elizabeth into our home.

Despite warnings from our colleagues, Moe and I were in complete agreement that we should take Elizabeth. By now we both were developing considerable confidence in our ability to handle the children. Dennis, Rosita and John were all doing well. And neither of us would consider the possibility that this appealing child was hopelessly ill. Fortunately for us, the other kids all liked Elizabeth and found her childishness and naïveté attractive, and they willingly assumed responsibility for helping us with her care.

As Dennis continued to progress through his regression and reached the ten-twelve-year-old period when father-son relationships are so important, both he and Moe began to make an effort to resolve their differences, and relate more to one another. Moe took advantage of their new intimacy by assuming a more active role in dealing with him. One of the first problems he tackled was the beard. Moe, who was also wearing a beard then, told Dennis that men were allowed to have beards, but that at his regressed age Dennis was still a child and it made us uncomfortable that his appearance was so inconsistent with his regressed age. Although he had been hysterical when we tried to get him to shave it off before, now Dennis agreed to sacrifice his beard for his father.

The day he did finally shave off his beard, we had all been invited to Charlottesville to a party. When Moe and Rosita and I stopped at Dennis's apartment to pick him up, he was so upset about the loss of his beard that we decided to send Rosita on ahead, and we both stayed with Dennis.

I was surprised to see how handsome Dennis was clean-shaven. Several times he had told me that he didn't want to shave his beard because his chin was ugly.

"You've got a good chin, Dennis," I remarked, while Moe was momentarily out of the room. "It's strong and well-molded. You have no reason to worry about people seeing your chin."

Dennis looked startled, and then said, "Will you stroke my chin?"

I reached over and caressed his cheek and chin. As I touched him, he began to tremble.

"What's wrong, Dennis?" I asked him.

"I liked that!" Dennis whispered, his tone guilty. "It stimulated me. I must have asked you to do it because I knew I'd like it—" He looked at me, his eyes contrite.

At that moment Moe joined us, and I said to him, "Dennis just asked me to stroke his chin—and now he's worried that he was being seductive—"

Moe burst out laughing.

Dennis looked relieved. He reached up, fingered his smooth chin tentatively. "Do you think it's all right to let other people see me like this—?"

"You look very handsome, Dennis," I told him. "It's a pleasure to see your face. Other people will enjoy seeing you, too."

He turned to me. "But they'll see what I'm *feeling*—"

"You don't have to hide what you're feeling, Dennis," Moe told him. "You have nothing to hide. It's all right for people to see your face."

"People who already know you will be glad to see what you really look like," I told Dennis. "And people who have never seen you before will like what they see. You have a good face, Dennis."

After an hour or so, Dennis seemed sufficiently reassured to go to the party with us. It was like a debut for him.

At this time Dennis began to develop some tentative interest in girls, and his relationship with Rosita began to take on a new perspective. We were uncomfortable with the slowly budding romance, but uncertain of how to deal with the problem, or even whether we had a right to take a stand. Both youngsters were so confused and timid about sex that we were afraid anything we might say would be experienced by them as a "sex-is-not-all-right" message.

Later we were to learn that sick kids, getting well, are not so easily discouraged from a drive as normal and healthy as sex, and our reluctance to establish clearly designated guidelines in this all-important area was a major mistake.

As Dennis was growing older in his regression, Moe and I became more aware of the depth and significance of the feelings we all were sharing and we began to realize that the relationship with us involved more permanence than we had first imagined. Dennis had often called me "Mommy" in babyish moments, but now he began calling us Mom and Dad.

One night as I put him to bed, he asked if we would adopt him. I was startled and said I would talk to Moe. After discussing it at length we told Dennis that if he still wanted us to adopt him after he was well and discharged from treatment, that we would be glad to do it. From then on he always called us Mom and Dad just as Rickey and Tom did.

As Dennis approached the end of the regression, we encouraged him to consider what relationship he wanted to have in the future with his natural parents. While he was in out-patient treatment with me Dennis had made one trip to the West Coast to visit his family. After he came to us, I had telephoned his mother several times to keep her informed about what was happening or to try to get information—although she had been unable to contribute very much.

Dennis decided that he could not manage a trip to California alone and he asked his parents to come to Virginia to visit him.

Dennis's relationship with his father seemed especially complex. I knew he had little feeling for his mother, but that he both loved and hated the man who had unsuccessfully raised him and who he felt had introduced him to much of his pathology. It was further complicated by his father's heavy drinking, which meant that he could not be counted on to behave rationally at any particular time. One of his father's aberrations, Dennis told me, had to do with confusion between manliness and mutilation, and he had suffered a number of accidents (some of them, Dennis felt, had been self-inflicted or caused by accident-proneness) so that he had a wooden leg.

The afternoon that they were due to arrive in Fredericksburg we were all gathered in the living room, waiting, when the doorbell rang. I asked Dennis if he wanted to greet his parents alone first, but he said, "No."

He trailed me into the hall, then hung back uneasily behind me while I opened the door.

I caught my breath in surprise. Dennis is over six feet tall, but the huge, shaggy, blond-bearded man who filled our doorway was a giant. He stomped past me, into the house, without bothering with social amenities, and grasped his son's

shoulders in his powerful hands, staring search-
ingly at him.

"How're you doing, boy?" he demanded, with
a sidewise glance of distrust at me. His eyes, like
Dennis's during an episode, had the bright animal gleam of the paranoid.

I turned back to the door to greet Dennis's
mother and ten-year-old sister, both of whom
had been ignored by the large, aggressive man
who took the initiative in introducing himself
and had then swept on into the living room,
with Dennis trailing him.

Dennis's mother was a plump, rather ordi-
nary-looking, fortyish matron with cool, opaque
brown eyes and an unruffled manner. It was
obvious that she was not upset by her husband's
lack of civility.

In the living room, Dennis's father surveyed
the scene, then carefully chose a seat for himself
against the wall in the corner, where he had a
full view of everything happening. He began to
chatter in a loud bluff stream of words, seldom
waiting for a reply, while at the same time sizing
us all up with covert suspicion. I saw his puzzled
eyes travel over Dennis's clean body and shaven
face. When he looked at me it was obvious that
he felt threatened, and he soon began to refer
to me as "that woman."

The other children watched him uneasily.
Dennis, who had remained standing until his
mother, sister, and I were seated, now chose a
chair between Moe and me.

I introduced the serious conversation. "Dennis has a lot to talk to you about," I told his

parents. "A lot has changed since he saw you last."

Dennis began with difficulty. Then, with support from Moe and me, he tried to tell his parents about his sickness, his fright and loneliness, their contributions to his pathology. Then he said, "I guess what I want most to talk to you about is the kind of relationship I can have with you now."

"Anything you want, son," his father said.

Dennis went on haltingly, explaining that he had little feeling for his mother. He barely remembered her. But he told her he appreciated what cooperation she had given me in providing information which was helping him to get well.

"My feelings toward you," he said, turning to his father, "are a lot more important to me." He tried to tell his father that since their relationship had contributed to his getting sick, now, in order to get well, he needed a new father. But he would like to continue to have some contact with his natural father—although it would have to be a different sort than they had shared before.

"Whatever is best for you, son," the big man said. "I've always loved you. You'll always be my son."

Dennis, who was by now in tears, rose spontaneously, crossed the room to his father and the two embraced.

The first part of the visit ended on that surprisingly amicable note, and Dennis's family went back to their hotel, planning to return that evening.

A few hours later, before they were due back, there was a telephone call for Dennis from his father. Sensing trouble, I followed him and listened while he took the call.

I had no difficulty hearing Dennis's father. He had been drinking and his voice, which was normally loud, was at shouting pitch. He was demanding that Dennis see him alone. Dennis was adamant that he would not do that, and that his father should come back to our house, as planned.

There was a shouting exchange between them, climaxed by Dennis yelling to his father, "If you came three thousand miles to see me, you can damn well come a few fucking more miles! I won't be bullied by you!"

"What did you say?" his father's voice roared over the telephone. "You called me a cock sucker!"

"I did not!" Dennis protested.

"Why did you call me that? That's no goddam way for a son to talk to his father!"

"I never called you that!" Dennis yelled back at him. "I never used that word in my life!"

Dennis had told me that his father had a trick of using a delusion to set up a fight. In the past, Dennis had always backed down. But now he was fighting back and denying the accusation. Dennis had learned not to play his father's game.

I took the phone away from Dennis and tried to quiet the shouting, angry man. After a brief unsuccessful skirmish, I hung up.

Dennis's mother and sister returned that

evening alone. I had been eagerly looking forward to talking about Dennis's infancy and growing up. I was disconcerted at how little his mother knew. To most of my questions, such as when was he toilet-trained, did he have colic, etc., she said, "I really don't know about that. You'll have to ask his father." Then she explained to me that when she went to the hospital to have her next baby, she had gone suddenly, and Dennis, who was left with neighbors, had been frightened. When she returned home he was angry and negativistic, and it was therefore easy to turn him over to his father while she gave her attention to the new baby girl. She seemed to have little or no recall of her son's behavior or development while he was growing up.

Yet she was unwilling to give him up. Sadly, she told me that in making the trip to Virginia she had hoped that we might agree to "give him back."

"I need them too much," Dennis told his mother. "I love them more than anybody. I want them to adopt me."

"Adopt you?" His mother turned to her daughter, who had sat silently throughout this exchange. "How would you like that?"

The little girl shifted uneasily, and then murmured, "Not much, I don't think—"

While we were sitting together in the TV room, several more telephone calls came in from Dennis's father. He was demanding to talk to Dennis. When the children who took the calls refused to interrupt us and call Dennis to the phone, he became threatening.

"If you don't get my boy to this phone," he finally roared at John, who had taken the last call, "I'm going to come over there and tear that fucking house off that fucking hill!"

In a few minutes he did arrive, stomping into the house without bothering to knock. We were still closeted in the small TV room which he had not seen on his earlier visit, and he did not find us. He toured the living room, dining room and kitchen, without finding any of his family, and then paused, apparently mystified by the whole thing. At this point Moe intercepted him, and guided him outside to the parking area, to attempt to reason with him.

A few moments later, there was a telephone call for me from one of the park rangers who patrol nearby Battlefield Park, and often stop by our house for a visit and coffee.

"Hey, Jacqui," the ranger said, "we just went by your place and Moe's out in the yard with a guy who's acting really crazy. We wondered if you needed help."

"We are having some difficulties," I admitted.

"It's outside our jurisdiction," the ranger said, "but I'll be glad to get a city car over there."

"Don't do anything until I check with Moe," I told him. "I'll let you know if we need help."

I hesitated to escalate the problem by sending in reinforcements, but I decided something should be done, and I sent one of the big boys outside.

Soon the three of them came back into the

house, led by the raging man who was still insisting that he see his son. They joined us in the TV room.

Dennis tried to talk to his father. He apologized for swearing at him. But his father ignored his efforts to make peace, and drunkenly continued to accuse Dennis of calling him the offensive name.

"And I had thought everything was going so well," Dennis finally said sadly, referring to the earlier visit.

"Well! Like hell it was!" his father snorted. "You put me in that chair and let those people give me the third degree, shining lights in my eyes, and telling me lies—"

Moe was trying, with intermittent success, to calm our unruly guest, and for some reason Dennis's father seemed to respond to Moe, although he obviously felt hostile to me. At one point while Moe was trying to soothe him, he turned to Dennis and said, "He's okay, he is. But he's got himself hooked up with that goddam fucking Jewess!"

"You say another thing like that and I'll throw you out!" Moe threatened. By now he was angry, too, and it looked as though violence was imminent. I was sorry I had turned down the ranger's offer to send help.

Dennis's father, however, had no interest in fighting with Moe. It was his son he was after. He suddenly turned on Dennis, thrust his size thirteen fists under his son's nose in a threatening gesture and said, "You called me names. Let's have it out now!"

It was obvious Dennis was not going to back down and I jumped between them, blocking the attack by throwing my arms around Dennis's neck at the same time that Moe grabbed his father.

The fight averted, we managed to get Dennis's parents and sister out of the house and on their way, and on that chaotic note the visit ended.

Now we would not consider letting ourselves or one of the children in for such a disastrous encounter. Parents are made to understand before a child comes to us that as he gets well his loyalties to us will take precedence over his previous family relationships.

Bizarre as this set of parents appeared to be, Moe and I were to learn that they were not actually atypical of the parents of schizophrenic children. We have usually found a serious disturbance in the mother's involvement with the child: indifference or detachment. We also often find that one or both parents are themselves seriously disturbed. In 50 percent of the families, one of the parents has had psychiatric hospitalization.

In the beginning, when we first took Dennis into our house, and then Rosita and John, we had no idea of the depth and permanence of the involvements we were undertaking with the children. I had often braced myself against the day when they would leave us, and return once again to their natural families.

But now I began to realize that if the children were to get well and stay well, that day would never come.

Chapter Six

ONE OF THE REASONS Elizabeth's family remained ignorant of the seriousness of her illness was her at-home behavior. For the most part, she had shown her parents only one face of her highly complex personality. Elizabeth could be so vigorously sweet-and-good that to anyone with any clinical experience, her behavior at those times was a caricature of infantile seductiveness. To the uninitiated, however, such behavior could be pleasing. Elizabeth's mother would invariably say at some point in any discussion with me, "Oh, but Elizabeth couldn't possibly have done that! She's such a *good* child!"

Elizabeth had also picked up her parents' habit of denial with a vengeance. When she was on the verge of a violent episode, which we could see was coming by the way she jiggled and giggled, I would say to her, "Elizabeth, what's wrong?"

She would reply, "Nothing. Nothing is wrong. Absolutely nothing. I feel perfectly *FINE!*"

And then off she'd go, into a convulsive rage.

When Elizabeth acted out, it didn't look the same as when Dennis acted out an episode, or Rosita, or anyone else I had observed. It really did look like a convulsion, with froth at the mouth and apparently involuntary muscular contortions. When the episode passed, she had no memory of what she had done during it, although she was able to talk about what had initially triggered the rage. It was obvious that she could kill either herself or someone else during such an episode without any awareness of what she was doing.

Elizabeth was not regressed in the usual sense. When she came to us she had practically no functional behavior to her personality. But neither had she regressed back to infancy, as Dennis had done. It was difficult to see where she was, beyond totally crazy. She was constantly beset with delusions and fantasies, was often completely out of touch with reality. Besides being extremely suicidal, she was likely to take a sudden notion that she could fly, or walk through glass.

She carried a large, smooth stone in her hand all the time, telling us it was her "holding stone" and refusing to let go of it.

One day I found her scrunched into a curious semicircle, with her head imprisoned between her knees. "What in the world are you doing?" I asked.

"I'm turning into a stone," she told me, without stirring.

"Why?"

"Stones don't feel!"

"But you aren't a stone," I said to her. "You're a little girl and you have to feel!"

Reluctantly she uncurled and looked at me,

her large eyes swimming with tears. "I can *too* be a stone!" she argued.

"Elizabeth," I said, "stones are inanimate objects. They don't have any feelings. Inanimate objects can't feel."

"That's right," she agreed happily. "That's why I want to be a stone!"

"You aren't an inanimate object," I told her. "You're a girl and you can't avoid feeling! Girls always feel!"

"I am?" she said sadly. "They do?" As usual, she could not argue long.

Being—or becoming—a stone was one of her most persistent delusions. When we took her to the clinic for Dr. Reed to check her out, she would not leave the house unless she was allowed to take her stone with her. She held it throughout the examination.

Her overadaptability was also a problem because Elizabeth was inevitably willing to accommodate herself to anything that anyone else said or did. She was a perfect patsy for reinforcing the other youngsters pathology. At that time we had with us temporarily a local girl, Susan, who shared a misperception common to many schizophrenics, that there was a transparent obstruction between herself and the rest of the world (the wall-of-glass syndrome). Susan called this her "plastic bag" and when she became angry or frightened she retired inside this imaginary structure, and refused to relate to any of us. One day when Susan was upset she announced that she was going to "take my teddy bear and get inside my plastic bag and never come out?"

Elizabeth went right along with the proposal. "Oh, that's a good deal!" she answered enthusiastically. "Then no one can ever hurt you!"

Susan, puzzled by this reaction, repeated, somewhat questioningly, "—and never come out?"

Elizabeth nodded. "Then you'll be safe," she encouraged Susan. "Just you and your teddy bear. How marvelous!"

"If you loved me, you wouldn't want me to go inside a plastic bag forever!" Susan said indignantly.

To Elizabeth's bewilderment, everyone was angry with her for what she had said to Susan.

"But she wanted to," Elizabeth wailed. "She said she wanted to!"

"You are responsible for the things you say and do," we told Elizabeth.

"I am?" she asked in utter amazement. This was apparently an entirely new concept to her, and one with which she was to have many painful encounters before she was well.

Elizabeth had to be kept under constant surveillance and it was in caring for her that we developed the system of supervision and restraining which we still use. One child was assigned to be with her at all times, to watch her and then call for help should anything happen. This is what we call "suicide supervision"—as opposed to "living-room supervision" which only requires that the babies or youngsters with behavior problems be watched when they are outside the living areas—a job which one staff person, or older child, can do for several children at once.

Elizabeth's attempts to kill herself occurred daily and seemed unrelated to anything that had just happened, or even to her mood at the time, which made them difficult to anticipate. The suicidal impulses usually followed occasions when she was angry. But the event that upset her may have happened hours (or even years) before. Later we were to relate this suicidal behavior to her homicidal impulses. When she was upset she often turned her anger on herself in preference to hurting others.

She was extremely strong for her size and when she was upset she bit and scratched, hurting herself and anyone else available. It normally took six strong people to hold her down in a chair. She would struggle frantically for fifteen or twenty minutes and then would calm down and tell us what was happening.

Although beating up people had been a frequent diversion, Elizabeth, ironically, was terrified by the prospect of being spanked. We all spelled out the house rules to her. But she had to test them for herself and find out if we really meant what we said.

She came to us with a long record of stealing. As she was growing up she periodically had made forays into department stores and carried off a hundred dollars' worth of merchandise at a time. She had been stealing for years.

I wish I didn't steal. It makes me feel like such a bad person. Once I told my older sister I had stolen a lot of junk from a jewelry store and I even showed it to her, in hopes she'd tell my parents. I wanted them to know what I was

*doing so they would make me stop. But they
never said a word....*

It's a constant surprise to us to find how
many middle-class children have never been
taught not to steal. Yet, it seems to me far simpler to punish a five-year-old for stealing (and
most children go through a stealing period at
five to six years of age) than it is to say, "That
isn't nice, dear," and then be confronted with a
fourteen-year-old who steals. When Moe and I
eventually did meet with Elizabeth's parents,
and discussed the stealing incidents, they said,
"We knew about it, but we thought she would
outgrow it. Lots of kids go through stages like
that."

This was yet one more instance of the parents' denial of an entire aspect of their daughter's behavior.

"What would you do if I stole something?"
Elizabeth asked me one day after she had been
with us several months and was beginning to be
somewhat functional. "Is it true that you'd
spank me if I stole?"

"Yes," I told her. "First of all I would spank
you. And then I would make you take the item
back to the store, and apologize to the owner."

I knew that it would not be long before Elizabeth would test me to see if what I said would
prove true. It was only days later, following our
conversation, that I took three of the girls shopping with me.

I usually do take one or more of the children
with me when I go out to do errands. They like
getting out of the house and it gives them extra

time alone with me which they need. Also I feel that it is a good thing for the community to see us together as a family, observing how my children behave.

I had never had any public behavior problem so far, and I did not anticipate that I would now. Our household is run on stricter lines than most and the children all know what I expect of them in public. Their anger, hostilities and rebellion are usually handled at home.

Later that day, after we were back home, Elizabeth and one of the girls who had been with me became very upset. "I'm bad! I'm so bad!" Elizabeth moaned. "Please let me die!"

The other girl was medicated and put to bed. Later she roused herself enough to stumble into the living room and tell us what had happened.

In the store that afternoon she had seen Elizabeth pick up and hide a compact. When the children were alone, she accused Elizabeth of stealing, saying, "If you don't tell, I will."

"I'll tell," Elizabeth promised.

The afternoon passed and the girl became more and more upset, waiting for Elizabeth's confession. Meanwhile, Elizabeth had completely forgotten the stealing as the event which precipitated her feelings of "being so bad."

Finally, confronted with the stealing, the sweet-faced child looked at me innocently. "Oh," she said, "I did?" When the stolen article was retrieved from her possession, she quite suddenly remembered the theft. "I wanted it," she explained. "I just took it because I wanted it!"

I led the still unbelieving girl into my room

and administered a sound spanking. She didn't cry, but afterward kept saying, "Oh wow! Oh wow! I never thought you'd *spank* me!" Her other parents had never, she said, punished her for anything. They told her about how *terrible* parents were for spanking their children. "They just made me feel evil and guilty," she said. "They never made me stop anything!"

The next day I took her back to the store and had her return the stolen merchandise to the stern-faced manager, with an apology. "I don't want you ever to come into my store again," he told her, "unless your mother is with you!"

The incident was discussed in the next Family Group, and the children decided, to avoid the confusion that had occurred between the girls, that in the future they would all consider it okay to tell on each other.

No one would be considered by the others to be tattling when he reported on another's behavior. They all knew that they were involved in each other's hope for health. The atmosphere was becoming charged with the desire to get well.

Elizabeth never stole again, but it was apparent that she was not through testing parental reactions to misbehaving. We wondered what she would do next.

"It'll be something in my department," Moe guessed. "She will want to be spanked by both parents before she's fully satisfied that we mean what we say."

Elizabeth selected running away as the means to test Moe. She was not at all interested in actually getting away from us, but she knew that that is something Moe always handled. She announced at breakfast one June morning that she was going to do it.

"If you run away, you know what you'll get, don't you?" Moe reminded her. "A good spanking from me."

Elizabeth smiled. That was precisely what she wanted to hear. She was ready to test Moe's authority just as he had predicted that she would do. Just to be sure, she told us she would head for the golf course.

She had chosen a lazy summery Saturday afternoon. Moe was at home. Most of our neighbors were home, too, that day, enjoying their lawns and backyards and the park.

Elizabeth waited till late afternoon, when our house was relatively quiet and most of the children were busy, and then with a wave and a giddy laugh she darted barefoot out the back door.

As she got away, her long hair flying behind her like a sail with the wind in it, one of the children sounded the alarm, and a mob thundered in pursuit.

Elizabeth glanced back over her shoulder, delighted with the chase, then bounded like a faun from rock to rock, across the neighboring backyards, through flower gardens, zigzagging playfully, without destination, her head back, laughing. She skipped through the nearby park, then into the woods, through an adjoining back pasture that belonged to a farm. Elizabeth was not interested in losing her pursuers, but only in

keeping a tantalizing distance between herself
and them. For Elizabeth, the end was the object.

Reaching the far side of the farm pasture, she
came to a stone wall, lightly scaled it, and
dropped down, to find herself in the carefully
tended back garden behind a Georgian mansion.
At that particular moment the wealthy, elderly
owners were out in their backyard, playing a
sedate game of croquet with visiting friends.

When Elizabeth dropped down into the middle of their game, they looked up, startled, then
gasped in surprise as her pack of pursuers came
tumbling over their wall after her, like so many
breathless Humpty Dumptys. When she saw
them almost upon her, Elizabeth let out a merry
laugh and skipped over the nearest wicket and
ran out of the yard into the driveway, down the
road and through a corn field.

When they reached the second field, in a burst
of speed Dennis suddenly streaked past the others, gained on Elizabeth till he was alongside
her, threw a strong arm around her slender
waist, and tackled her, pulling her to a stand-
still. They both went down into a struggling
heap.

By then the other kids had reached them, and
grabbed an unresisting Elizabeth, while Rosita
came back to the house to fetch me.

As Rosita led me to where they waited, I
passed the elderly neighbors who were still
standing out in their yard, watching the chase
with considerable interest. When I reached the
children, they released Elizabeth to me and I

escorted her home, where she waited for her father. Dennis went back over her route to soothe the neighborhood.

Moe took Elizabeth into the office, sat her down and gave her a long lecture about running away, and why it was such a selfish thing to do to the rest of the family, and she apologized and cried a little and Moe held her and comforted her. And then when she was quiet and docile, and apparently thought that the scene was over and he had forgotten about the spanking, Moe said, "Okay, honey, let's go!"

Elizabeth's face dropped a mile. "Oh, Papa!" she protested, "You're not—?"

"Yes, I am!" And Moe turned her over his knee and gave her a thorough spanking.

Elizabeth cried a little more after that and said she would never run away again. And she didn't. She had found out what it meant to be punished by both parents, and for the first time she could believe that we would take care of her and that her "evil ways" would be dealt with.

Moe did not feel as easy about administering punishment as I did. I was with the children each day, while he had only evenings and week-ends with them, since he maintained a full-time job away from home. Round-the-clock exposure and constant crises had gotten me past feeling uncomfortable with the role of disciplinarian so that by now I did whatever I felt was necessary to handle a situation, without bothering to con- sider whether it was the "best" possible thing I could do. But Moe still had some qualms about his actions. He admitted to me that at times he still felt more like a "social worker playing father" than he did like a real father.

We both worked under the obvious handicap of knowing that with one's own children you have time on your side to correct mistakes, but with our sick children, the messages we gave them, and the punishment we dealt out, had to be 90 percent right because they would never pass this way again. This was their last chance—a responsibility that gave each of us occasional bad moments.

At about the same time that we took Elizabeth, Moe received an appeal from a totally unexpected quarter when a close friend called him about his own son.

Moe had known the boy, Mark, since he was a baby, and I had met him when we visited in his parents' home. Neither Moe nor I were aware that the boy was in trouble.

The family appeared close-knit. The parents seemed proud of their son and had told us a lot about his achievements and had happily sent him off to college the previous year. Mark was a good-looking boy in a dark, brooding sort of way, muscularly built, with heavy, black wavy hair and dark-brown eyes. He had some musical and acting talent and a "golden boy" script from his mother. There was every reason to think he would have an exciting and successful future.

Quite the opposite happened. Mark had nothing more to offer than hundreds of other boys from other middle-class families who were alone and lost in a big city. Far from the golden boy of his parents' dreams, he was just another strange kid in a small room at a huge, faceless university. He was frightened. He was lonely. He began to panic. But when he called his parents midterm and tried to get across his fears to them, they did not suggest that he come home. So he stayed. And the longer he stayed, the sicker, more frightened and confused he became.

By the time Mark's father called Moe, the family was aware that their son was not doing well. He was not attending classes. He was determined to leave college altogether, take his guitar and bum around the country. They asked if we would take a look at him. When we agreed to do so, they persuaded Mark to drop in and visit us. He looked good when he walked in the door. But he was hallucinating before he left, sending out very urgent messages that he was sick. He did test out to be a paranoid schizophrenic.

When we reported this to Mark's parents, they asked us if we would take their son. We told them we would indeed like to help Mark. But we warned them that if we did agree to take him, it would have to be with the same sort of understanding that we had with our other children. Despite the fact they were close friends, they would have to be willing to give their son to us. Their relationship with him might never be the same again.

Both of Mark's parents were understandably upset by his illness, and desperately eager for him to get well. "No matter what it takes," they assured us, "it's all right with us. Just so you will help him."

"But if he does get well," I warned his mother, "he may be part of our family, not yours."

"It doesn't matter," she said. "Do whatever is necessary. The only thing in the world we want for him is to be healthy again."

Moe and I agreed to take Mark—we were both fond of him anyway, and wanted to help—but with some reluctance. It was difficult enough to cope with strange parents, and try to make them understand what we had to do, but the prospect of explaining to close friends how they had failed to provide adequate parenting for their son was a situation we didn't like to face.

For a while, even after we took Mark, Moe simply refused to face the truth about the boy's condition. He was so fond of Mark's father, he could not accept the fact that his friend might have contributed to the boy's illness. For weeks, he denied how sick Mark really was.

Finally I was forced to have it out with him. "Look at his behavior and tell me what you think," I demanded.

"I think he's sick," Moe admitted.

"He is, Moe, very sick," I told him. "You can't deny it, no matter how much you think of his parents. This kid is *sick*. And you are not going to be able to help him until you accept the fact that he is."

"All right," Moe's voice was heavy with resignation. "You're right. I guess I just didn't want to believe it."

"Until you believe it and until you are willing

to be a father to him, he's not going to get well,"
I warned him.

In a sense it seemed presumptuous for Moe to
take over the role of Mark's father from his own
friend, yet we had seldom seen a boy who was
hungrier for male parenting. Mark did not regress, but he was dependent on us and the
household to protect him from a world with
which he could not cope.

As an infant he had been taken by his parents
to Israel and lived in a kibbutz. We don't know
what happened to him there, but his shallow
involvement with other people and the development of asthma, which he used as a game to
insure mothering, dated from that period. Because of his poor relationship with his father, he
had a sexual identity problem. He felt extremely
inadequate and incompetent. As a youngster in
high school, he had been seduced by an older
man, a teacher, just at a time when he was
seeking to establish sexual identity and the experience had shattered his fledgling masculine
self-confidence. That, added to parental expectations and ambitions which he was totally incapable of fulfilling, had left him feeling confused,
insecure and thoroughly frightened. Besides
working out his emotional problems, he very
much needed a father figure to confide in and to
emulate.

Eventually Moe was able to relate to Mark as
a father without self-consciousness. He was able
to talk easily to the boy in a fatherly fashion,
and gradually a warm, companionable bond developed between them.

Each evening, when Moe turned into our drive, he automatically braced himself for "whatever kind of hell is waiting for me tonight." Since we deal so vigorously with everyone's pathology, walking into the living room always means wading knee-deep in powerful emotions of hate, anger, fear—and also love. Moe never knew what might be happening until he opened the door. And he worried a good deal about whether he would be adequate to meet whatever situation confronted him.

One night he came home to total chaos. Elizabeth was upset and some of the kids were trying to deal with her. Tom was shouting at Dennis, who was trying to frighten everyone into submission by out-yelling them. One of the girls was struggling in restraints and Rickey was crying.

"Make him stop!" Tom demanded of his father, indicating Dennis, who certainly seemed to be the source of much of the confusion. And Moe, without waiting to find out what was going on, smacked Dennis. "You stop bullying people!" he said.

Dennis was furious. He accused Moe of being grossly unfair for punishing him before he had found out what was really going on. "I was helping," he insisted, "and you punish me!"

Later, after everything had quieted down, and we had all had supper, Moe was sitting out on the front steps in the late spring dusk, with Mark at his side. He was pondering what had happened.

"I didn't handle it correctly," he mused aloud to himself. "A situation like that makes me feel so damned inadequate. I felt I had to do something—fast. But I didn't stop to find out what it was all about. I just smacked him—like I would a kid of my own—because on the face of it it looked like he was causing a lot of the commotion. I wonder if I have the right to haul off and smack a kid like that—?"

"But, Dad," Mark interrupted softly, "if you don't do it, who else is going to do it? You're our father and you have the right. There's no one else. You're the end of the line."

Moe stared at Mark for a long moment, and then, as he said later, "everything suddenly fell into focus. I realized that if this boy—or any of the others—was going to get well I was going to have to love him like a father loves his own son—and whack him when I thought he needed it, and hug him when I felt like it. Otherwise, he would never make it. And if he, and the other kids, were willing to believe I was their father and had a father's rights, then who was I to argue? If they believed in me and I believed in them, and I happened to guess wrong once in a while, we'd all still survive. . . . "

Moe gave Mark a grateful hug, straightened his shoulders and smiled. That was the turning point for him, the moment in which he changed from being a "social worker playing father" into a full-time father. After that he didn't waste time and energy worrying about whether he always did the correct thing. He just did the very best he knew how.

The children knew, even better than Moe and I did, that we represented their one chance.

They tried to help us over our low moments by showing a growing investment in each other. By now, Dennis was well enough so that he was able to give us considerable help in handling the sicker children. If he did misbehave, it was directed only at me. Rosita also could be helpful at times, although I could not depend on her in the same way, since her behavior was more variable. But the other children liked, and responded well, to her.

During her hospitalization Rosita had made friends with several other sick children, among them a sixteen-year-old Negro girl named Shirley, who lived in a rural section of Virginia, not far from us. I had not yet seen Shirley, although Moe had worked briefly with her while we lived in Charlottesville. She had been discharged from the hospital and was back home with her family.

I came home one afternoon, from a meeting at the clinic, to find the house in an uproar.

"Shirley's under Rosita's bed," Tom filled me in, "and none of us can get her out."

Rosita had told me that she was expecting a visit from Shirley that day so I was not surprised to find that the child was in the house. But I did not know the significance of her hiding under a bed. I knew little more than that she was schizophrenic.

I went into the girls' bedroom and got down on my hands and knees and peered under Rosita's bed.

Back against the wall crouched a pretty, chubby little black girl with big, glazed brown eyes, a loose, sensitive mouth and nappy black hair. I called to her, to reassure her, and told her to come out.

She did not respond.

I kept on talking to her, cajoling her with soft words and held out my arms. As I stared at that silent black baby, and felt my arms widen instinctively to receive her, I knew I could be this child's mother. It was a biological response. There are simply some children about whom I know, the moment I see them, that I will be able to take them into my arms and mother them.

I had never previously felt physically attracted to any black person. My contact with black people was fairly limited. But my attraction for this big-eyed girl was real and intense. I knew I could love her.

After a few more minutes of reassurances from me, she finally let me get hold of her and pull her out from under the bed. I sat a while on the floor, cradling her in my arms, and soothing her. She stared at me the whole while, her brown eyes slightly out of focus, her silence broken only by an occasional monosyllable, "mmm," "ymmmm." When she felt relaxed in my arms, I let her go. She got up and went to play with Rosita, and seemed to enjoy the rest of the weekend.

I frequently found Shirley at the house after that, and whenever I encountered her I experienced the same emotional exchange between us. I was strongly attracted to the child, a fact which she seemed to recognize, respond to—and at the same time, fear. Once, after she had visited us, and gone home, I found a note tucked under my bedroom door:

> Thank you for letting me come
> to visit you.
> I had lots of fun and
> Understood a bit more about myself too.
> Although some of the things
> were difficult to think about accepting,
> I will certainly give them a try.
> Thank you for making me feel wanted,
> Loved, and some good.
> I LOVE YOU

Shirley became attached to all the children, a familiar adjunct to our regular family. She felt at home with all of us and visited as often as she could. She also sought out our children where she went to high school in Charlottesville. Dennis was very fond of Shirley in a "big brother" sort of way and she obviously adored him. I cautioned her, however, that while it was all right to spend time with him at our house, I did not want her to see him at college. Mindful of Virginia racial tension, I specifically warned Shirley not to go to Dennis's apartment in Charlottesville. But one day she ignored my warning.

I'm in Dennis's room now. "Don't ever go to the boys' room," Jacqui said. But I've come anyhow. Because Dennis invited me to come. He's my favorite big brother, and he told me if I'd come to see him he'd teach me to play the guitar. .... Now he's showing me how to hold it— just so. He's got his hands over mine. There, the

*music is coming out of the strings, so pretty it
makes me happy. I love Dennis. . . .*

I received an emergency call from one of Dennis's friends.

"You better come quick. Something's happened between Dennis and Shirley. She's sitting here like a statue. She won't respond to any of us."

I dropped whatever I was about to do, and drove directly to Charlottesville. In anticipation of my arrival, Dennis had disappeared. I found Shirley sitting on the couch in a neighboring apartment with some youngsters trying to care for her. She was sitting absolutely still, immobile, staring off in space, her big eyes blank, unblinking. When I spoke to her, she made no response. She did not look at me and she did not appear to know I was there.

I tried, without success, to get her to speak to me. She remained immobile, registered nothing. She was obviously in no condition to tell me what had happened. I sent the boys out to find Dennis and bring him back to me.

Dennis eventually was found and told his mother wanted him. He arrived, sheepish, guilty, thoroughly frightened and very ashamed, since he also had been warned against entertaining Shirley. He told me that she had come to his apartment to take a guitar lesson. She had played well, and in what he insisted was not a sexual encounter, he had grabbed her and tried to kiss her forehead.

Shirley had frozen at his touch, and had neither moved nor spoken since then. Dennis appealed for help and, terrified when they couldn't pull her out of the episode, the youngsters decided the only thing to do was send for me.

For the first time it was apparent to me that Shirley was catatonic. I didn't know what to do. I had never dealt with catatonics and I did not know what it would take to pull her out of this unblinking silence, this paralysis of fright. But obviously I had to think of something. And quickly, too. I looked from the immobilized Shirley across to Dennis. He was trembling with fear. I knew his own hold on heterosexuality was still so new and tenuous that it could easily be irreparably damaged by a single bad encounter.

I sent Dennis and the other boys outside to wait. When they were gone I turned to Shirley.

"I told you that you were not to come to the boys' apartment without permission," I said in a severe voice. "And now here you are. Something has to be done about that!"

I pulled her stiff, unyielding body across my knee and began to spank her vigorously. With each blow I could feel the energy revitalizing her. I kept on until she was shrinking away from my hand, and had begun to cry.

"Please stop, I'll be good!" she gasped.

The silence was broken. When I let her go, she stood before me, her face tear-streaked, rubbing her bottom with both hands. She was still crying, but she was alert now, her eyes focused on me, obviously awaiting what I would say or do next.

"I expected more sensible behavior from you, Shirley," I scolded her. "No sixteen-year-old girl belongs in a boy's room unless she is prepared for him to make a pass at her. You provoked this. It's your fault. You are responsible for what happened. I don't ever want this to happen again."

"I won't do it again, I promise," Shirley sniffed, rubbing her tear-filled eyes with her fists. Now that she felt adequately punished, she had relinquished her paralyzing fright and was behaving normally.

I drove her to her own house, then continued on back to our house. On the drive home, I contemplated what I had just done and it occurred to me that it was probably as unusual a therapeutic encounter as any therapist had engaged in! I wondered what would happen if that pretty little black girl went home and reported how the white therapist had whipped her because a white boy had made a pass at her. How could I ever explain that?

Moe was distressed when he found that I had come home without bringing Dennis back with me. He felt that I should not have left the boy alone in the frightened condition that he was in. He was right. After I left him, Dennis borrowed a motorcycle and deliberately ran into a parked truck so that he injured his leg. When I went back to fetch him home the next day after we had heard about the accident, I found that he had done nothing to treat his leg and it was badly lacerated and swollen. He admitted, on the ride home, that he had hurt himself deliberately. He was very upset the previous day that I had punished Shirley for the incident but had failed to punish him. Since the incident had sexual overtones I had considered it a father-son matter, and I told Dennis that he needed to talk to his father, rather than to me, about it. It was up to Moe to provide Dennis with script for his future encounters with girls.

Dennis also admitted that he had figured if he hurt himself I would protect him from having to face a scene with his father. I refused to do this, and I suggested to Dennis that the inevitable talk with his father would proceed better if he could avoid being sullen.

Dennis was very frightened when we arrived home. But Moe made it clear to him that the confrontation should take place immediately and that night after everyone else had gone to bed, the three of us sat up, while Moe and Dennis had a long, late session. I was present but I did not intercede.

I had thought that perhaps Moe might blow up at the boy, but he was very cautious with Dennis, obviously anxious not to damage the boy's precarious sexual identification. Dennis cried some, but he handled the scene with his father quite well. The messages that Moe gave to him were that sex was all right, that he should not hurt people, and that he should avoid sick girls.

We had previously decided to let Dennis begin driving the cars, but Moe now grounded him indefinitely. Dennis was upset by this restriction, but he did not argue about it. He seemed more concerned about the fact that there was something left emotionally unresolved between him and his father. For the next few days Dennis stayed close to me, and we talked a great deal—and eventually what was bothering him came to light. In his free attitude toward Shirley, he had been imitating Moe's freedom with the sick girls. We then talked at length about the difference between a fathering relationship and a sexual relationship. For the first time Dennis seemed to understand that even when he was completely well, he would still be only a boy of twenty—and not a forty-five-year-old man.

We saw no more of Shirley for the next couple of weeks. And then one morning I got a call from a therapist friend of mine who lives in Charlottesville.

"I have Shirley here with me now," she told me. "She's in very bad condition and she has asked me to bring her to you."

Then my friend outlined briefly what had happened. The night before, Shirley's parents had gotten into a violent fight in front of the children, and at some point during the raging battle, her mother had pushed her father through a plate-glass window. The mother's arm had been badly cut, the father's back and head had been cut and there was a good deal of blood and commotion.

Shirley had become so terrified that she ran out into the night, found a telephone and simply called the nearest responsible adult that she knew, who happened to be my friend, and begged her for protection.

It was the middle of the night but my friend and her husband got up and drove out to the

place where Shirley had said she would be waiting for them, picked her up and brought her to
their home.

I instructed my friend to get in touch with the
police, and explain what had happened, and then
bring Shirley to me.

She drove to Fredericksburg the next day, and
delivered to me a very sick, very angry, very
frightened little girl.

Chapter Seven

WHEN THE WORD GOT around among our friends that we had taken Shirley into our household, we received a barrage of distressed calls and letters. We were living in a middle-class white development in a southern state at a time when racial tensions rocked the countryside. "What you are already doing is unusual," warned a friend who was a professional in the community, "that the idea of adding the race problem on top of it is simply ridiculous! You will get so much opposition now that you won't be able to function at all!"

But there was Shirley, already knowing that I would be her mother, climbing into my lap, making sucking motions with her mouth, clinging to me with urgent, infant hands. Like Dennis, Shirley went back into her babyhood in confused, inconsistent sequences. Like him, she would not go to sleep until I had come in to kiss her goodnight.

Shirley regressed even further back into infancy than Dennis had—back to an unborn state, to those early beginning moments of life when the infant is still sheltered securely within the mother's body, quiet and safe, nurtured and cushioned from every threat—even from its mother's irrationality or irresponsibility, beyond the reach of her anger, protected by a benign nature.

I don't know what getting born had meant to Shirley the first time it happened. But as she grew up, she found herself belonging to an impoverished Negro family where there was not enough of anything to go around. Shirley's earliest memories are of being hungry and unfed, frightened and without comfort, angry and mistreated. She grew up thinking, over and over again, "I wish I had never been born."

The problem in treating catatonics, such as Shirley, is to convince them that it is advantageous to be born again. This can be very difficult to do, because before the patient allows himself to be reborn he must be persuaded that the world is not the hostile, ugly place he previously experienced, nor mothering the arbitrary relationship he once knew. We had no way of knowing how much love, care, and good family experiences it would take before Shirley would be willing to relinquish her fear and decide that she could make a place for herself in the world.

Shirley was not withdrawn all the time, like those silent, waxlike figures one sees sitting immobilized in mental hospitals who seem so completely out of contact with the world. She had catatonic episodes, and then, at other times, was active and expressive. She wanted very much to go to school, so we worked it out that she got up in the morning with other school children and attended school for half days. She was too regressed to read, but she was able to follow the lessons by having other children read them to her. By mid-afternoon, however, she was usually raging in restraints or withdrawn into sullen silence trying to withdraw into a closet or corner, sitting with her eyes out of focus.

The first time Shirley acted out the scene of her conception and birth, the ring of children watched in fascination—and some terror—while she pantomimed her creation and entrance into the world. The round red velvet bolster from the sofa became her father's penis. The curved sectional sofa was her mother. She pushed the bolster back and forth under the sofa, demonstrating intercourse, and then she crawled into the dark recess beneath the sofa, becoming a fetus before our eyes, curling into a ball, helpless, yet protected from the world. Finally she began the long, tortuous struggle, squirming, writhing, gasping for breath as she emerged from the birth canal and air replaced the fetal fluids in her mouth, and she arrived in the outside world at last, howling and angry.

Then, while we were still sitting, staring at her, stunned by the vivid, explicit scene, Shirley's eyes, which had been closed or swimming in fantasy throughout the pantomime, suddenly came into sharp, hard focus. She looked around desperately for a means of escape, and then, before we could collect ourselves to stop her, she suddenly vaulted, from an almost sitting position in the center of the room, up over the couch, clearing the heads of those on it, and was out of the room and down the hall before we realized what she was doing.

Fortunately, John Christy, our son-in-law, had come in late and taken a chair outside the circle. While the rest of us were still stumbling over one another, he was able to follow and grab her before she got out the back door. She struggled frantically, but he succeeded in holding her until some of the others arrived. They dragged her, struggling and crying, to my lap. Warm milk was already prepared, and I held and stroked and fed her until she was calm in my arms.

I want you to hold me, but I am so afraid. When you touch me I am afraid, for nothing before felt comforting about a mother's touch.

As Shirley repeated the acting out of her birth, we began to help her resolve the fearful question of whether she was to be or not to be. The relationship with me was all-important, and while she discounted everyone else, somehow she always managed to let me know that if I continued to love her and care for her long enough, she could get well. A baby must be welcomed by its mother, who holds it and loves it and feeds it and shows through all the familiar symbols of mothering that the world is potentially a warm and loving and not always a hostile and frightening place.

It was because of Shirley's eating problems that I began using a bottle to feed the regressed babies. It had not occurred to me with Dennis, but with Shirley the need could not be ignored and we could not have fed her otherwise. When unborn, she would suck but could not swallow at all, but the newly born Shirley would swallow if she were offered a baby bottle. I bought a supply of baby bottles and began to prepare milk made up with powdered food supplements which could be heated quickly. Later we found that this symbol of nurturing was comforting to many of the children and we began to use it freely when anyone seemed to want it.

Frequently Shirley varied her birth scene with an equally terrifying reenactment, also in pantomime, of the gruesome battle between her parents the night she ran away from home.

She was vacuuming the rug in the girls' bedroom one day, when she suddenly called her sister Barbara, who had recently joined the family, to come and watch. Shirley seemed quite excited and she put the vacuum cleaner in the center of the room, and announced to the puzzled Barbara, "That's my father!"

Then she began reenacting the fight, leaping from one position to another as she played first her father attacking her mother, then her mother attempting to dodge the attack, and finally, her own small, frightened self, trying desperately to get out of the way. She hid under the table. Then her mother dragged her out and used her as a shield against the father's blows, whereupon the father began hitting Shirley.

Shirley grabbed one of the tubes from the cleaner and began beating herself furiously across the arm. "This is my father," she screamed. "He's killing me!"

Barbara was frightened and had no idea what to do. At first she had thought Shirley was playing, then she realized the game was deadly serious. Tentatively she tried to put her hand on

Shirley to soothe her. Shirley struck out angrily at her, then jumped up onto the bed, curled into a fetal position and pulled the covers up over her head.

Barbara ran out and called for help.

When they finally managed to pull Shirley out of the bed and onto the floor, she struck out wildly at anyone who touched her.

And all the while she sobbed piteously, "I want me! I want Shirley. Where is Shirley? Please get me Shirley!"

If only we could. But the self that Shirley sought was still not available, to her or to any of us.

Time after time Shirley cut herself, hacking at her arms with knives or broken glass. Once, one of the boys caught her out at the garbage can, industriously hacking at her arm with the raw edge of a newly opened tin can.

In spite of constant supervision she was often successful in making deep gashes in her arms; today she has a long line of scars between her wrist and elbow. She did not seem to be trying to kill herself, but when she succeeded in cutting herself she viewed the blood with morbid fascination.

We never learned what actually happened with Shirley's parents, but we knew she always felt torn between them. In her fantasies her mother was always trying to kill her because her father loved her better, and much of her panic and running away was an effort to escape her mother's vengeance. At night she was always afraid to go to sleep for fear someone would kill her.

Shirley's fantasies about older men, her father's age, all had to do with sex and murder. On several occasions she included in her pantomime a sequence in which she was molested by an older man. Her relationship with Moe was, at first, very confused. She seemed to desire his love and attention but since she did not know what a healthy paternal role was, she showed her feelings for him by being seductive. When Moe refused to respond to her advances, she became angry with him.

I want you to touch me like you touch my sisters. I want you to hold me and to stroke me. But I fear you. I fear all men. And fathers are my greatest fear of all.

Shirley's body, medium in height, round and well shaped, gave little clue as to her extraordinary physical strength and agility. Her strength was not a manifestation of her psychosis, as it was with many of the children. She was as strong and vigorous in her play as she was at times she was upset, and she was sometimes indispensable in controlling other children's acting out. Humiliating as it was to the boys, Shirley was as strong as any of them, and it always took several to control her. It was with Shirley that Moe finally faced the predicament he had feared with Dennis. In their first disciplinary encounter, Shirley refused to be punished by her father and, much to Moe's embarrassment, took triumphant possession of his belt.

Shirley obviously delighted in such incidents

and provoked Moe constantly. With me she was more docile. Several times when the boys were unable to handle her struggles, I was able to control her. Although she never hesitated to bite, hit, kick or otherwise injure anyone else who tried to hold her, she would not risk hurting me. My welfare was obviously too important to her survival.

Sometimes Shirley simply gave up on the world that confused and frightened her; then if someone wasn't quick enough to intercept her she was off and running, wildly, aimlessly, into the street, the road, the town. We were all afraid that Shirley might either deliberately kill herself or accidentally get herself killed before we could catch and protect her. Once when the boys lost sight of her, a police prowl car spotted them, and slowed down to ask what the trouble was. When Dennis explained they were trying to catch a sick girl before she did damage to herself, the police joined in the chase and succeeded in spotting Shirley, racing alongside a railroad track.

At another time, when she had exhausted our resources of physical endurance and Moe and the boys were wrestling her to the hospital emergency ward to get her sedated, she got free, jumped out of the car, and started running along the street with everyone chasing after her. They had nearly caught her when another car, filled with black men, cruised by, saw the pack of white men pursuing the fleeing black girl, and screeched to a sudden stop alongside Shirley, obviously prepared to defend her. For a tense moment it looked like the makings of a race riot.

Then Shirley took charge of the situation. "You go on—you hear!" she screamed. "You leave us alone. It's none of your business!"

Puzzled, the black men watched for a moment and then drove slowly on.

The combination of the two such wild, crazy girls as Shirley and Elizabeth in the same household at the same time proved to be almost more than we could handle. They were each fleet as young deer. And they were both dangerously suicidal. The main difference between them in behavior, at this time, was that while Elizabeth had no functional *behavior* to fall back on, Shirley could, if she decided to do so, pull herself together. Crazy as she was at times, she was always quiet and well-behaved in the classroom, and even without reading she was quite capable of absorbing her studies—a fact which was later dramatically brought home to us when to everyone's surprise, she graduated salutatorian of her class.

She could also, if she felt strongly enough about it, get control of herself in the middle of an upset and function effectively in an emergency. I was sitting in the big bedroom that the girls shared (we have double-decker bunks in both the boys' and the girls' rooms) talking to Elizabeth, Shirley and Rosita one evening after supper while a severe electrical storm crackled and exploded outside our windows. Suddenly, all the lights went out.

As we were hunting around for candles and matches, there was a light pad of racing feet. Then a second set of running steps followed them. At the other end of the house there was a loud crash and several screams.

We ran for the girls' bathroom; one of the boys was ahead of us with a flashlight. Elizabeth and Shirley were on the floor, locked in a wrestling embrace, rolling over and over in a bed of fractured glass, while Shirley shrieked for help.

When we pulled them apart and got them back on their feet, we found that both girls were badly cut. Later, bandaged and calmed, we got the whole story.

"When those lights went out I was thinking, man, if I felt like killing myself, this would sure be the time to do it!" Shirley explained with a droll grimace at Elizabeth. "I didn't just happen to feel like killing myself at the moment. But then I heard Elizabeth running out of the room. And I knew for sure what she was going to do. So I ran after her—"

By the time Shirley reached the bathroom Elizabeth had already seized the glass and smashed it over the wash basin. She was preparing to slash her wrists with the jagged edge when Shirley burst into the room, jumped on her, and the two girls went down together, the glass shattering beneath them. This was the side of Shirley's personality that made her so infinitely lovable—that she would go to such heroic extremes to save the life of someone she loved even though she had so little respect for her own.

All this violent activity was, unfortunately, not going unnoticed. Until this time the community was not much aware of what we were doing. However, Shirley's running away and several incidents involving other youngsters, began to call attention to our household. Reports Tom and Rickey brought home from school began to confirm this.

"The other kids keep asking me why I got so many crazy brothers and sisters," Rickey complained.

"There's a rumor going around that I live with a bunch of hippies," Tom added, with a laugh. Tom made it sound like some kind of compliment. But I wanted to check him out.

"Does that bother you?" I asked him.

"Not me," Tom shrugged. "I get more attention and have more kids to play with this way than if there was just Rickey and me."

"How about you?" I turned to Rickey. "Do you feel that way?"

"Aw, sometimes," Rickey shrugged, in a manful imitation of his older brother's laissez-faire attitude. "It is kind of nice to have the other guys here to play ball with. But sometimes, they're a *pain!*"

Tom tried to reason with his brother. "You can't have it both ways, Rick."

"I dunno." Rickey wandered off, grumbling to himself.

Tom's equilibrium was firmly in balance. But I knew that Rickey's was not. He fluctuated between enjoying extra playmates and being embarrassed when the children in school teased him about them.

I decided that we had to be seen in the community, as a family, more often. The more people saw of us, behaving acceptably in public, the

less of a threat we would be. The worst scenes,
from the standpoint of our public relations, were
when we were forced to haul struggling, screaming youngsters to the hospital. I wished that
there were a better, more effective way to handle
that problem.

Not long after my talk with Tom and Rickey,
Dr. Reed came to see Moe and me one evening
about the same subject. "I'm afraid you've got
to make some changes," he told us. "There's
entirely too much rumor and gossip going
around the community about you and the children."

Don told us that the town was afloat with
rumors: that we were a commune of hippies;
that we were sanctioning a drug scene; that we
were a communist plot. We told Don that the
worst problem, from our point of view, was that
whenever a youngster was acutely upset and
required medication we had no recourse but to
take him to the hospital emergency room, sometimes exposing him to dozens of curious bystand-
ers when he would appear at his worst. "Every
time any one of them is out of control, there's
nothing we can do but manhandle him all the
way to the hospital," I complained. "It's practically a public show."

"There's no reason for that kind of exposure,"
Don mused. "It isn't fair to you—or the community." He thought a moment. "I think I know
how we can handle it. You can enroll each child
in the clinic. Most of them are after-care patients anyway. Then they will be on record as
being under my care—which first of all will reas-

sure the community that they are receiving proper medical attention. Then, since I'll know them, in emergencies you can phone me. I can prescribe tranquilizers, concentrates. They will work fast and that should eliminate most of the hospital trips. You can sedate the children right here at home."

This proved to be a major turning point in our ability to care for the children. Once we had effective medication on hand at all times, and were able to administer it ourselves, there were few situations which we could not handle in the privacy of our own home.

There was also the problem of help in the house. David Rohrer, who had been working for us during the summer, was due to return to college in September and we were presented with several organizational problems. We considered whether Dennis could replace David. He had been unhappy living in Charlottesville the previous spring and was relieved to return home for the summer. We knew he was not eager to go back to live at school. As always, we were determined to keep him as functional as possible, and were unwilling for him to give up school and remain at home. However, if he took on responsibilities at home, we reasoned, he could have the support and security of being with us and still function at his best.

Dennis was pleased with the proposal and we finally agreed that he would commute to Charlottesville for one or two classes and also help at home.

We also decided that it was unrealistic for me

to work, and I quit my job at the Mental Health Clinic. Although I would continue to have a small private practice in Washington, D.C., I decided to devote my time almost entirely to the children and to the serious study of schizophrenia.

Before we got the household under smooth control, however, a petition for our eviction had already been circulated among our neighbors. The City Inspector appeared at Moe's office in town one morning and told him that we were in violation of zoning ordinances in that the area we lived in was restricted to private families and that we were running an institution.

"I'm sorry about this, Mr. Schiff," the Inspector told Moe, "but it looks as though you will have to move."

"The hell we will!" Moe roared. "The charge has to be proven first. And I am telling you that we are not an institution. We are a family. You can come and see for yourself."

"You must admit it's a rather unusual family," the Inspector smiled. "You have a lot more children than most families—"

"But they are our kids," Moe insisted stoutly. "We are not doctors. We are their parents. Someone is going to have to prove in court that we are not a family before I will listen to any petition—"

"All right, Mr. Schiff," the Inspector held up his hand placatingly. "I've heard a lot of good things about what you're doing. And I'll go back and report that you do not feel there is any justification for forcing you to move. We will see what your neighbors say to that."

It was at this point that our friends began to surface and we began to draw active support from the community. Many people in Fredericksburg, including the Mental Health Association, several public agencies, and our friends at St. George's Episcopal Church, the Reverend and Mrs. Faulker, came out in active support of what we were doing. Openly reinforcing our work, Mary and Tom Faulker took a seriously disturbed boy whom I was treating into their home and began to successfully reparent him along the lines on which we were working with our children.

Also, some of the children had already sold themselves to local townspeople and merchants. As the manager of a big drug store told me, "I like to see your kids come into the store, Mrs. Schiff. Because they are so much better behaved than the average teenager. We don't have to watch them."

We did not, as our friends had feared, run into trouble with the community because one of our children was black. Shirley herself, however, became acutely upset at the time of Dr. Martin Luther King's assassination in 1968, and the angry riots that followed. Fredericksburg held a memorial walk as a tribute to Dr. King, which was terminated by services at the St. George's Church, and we decided to take the whole family. I kept Shirley close to me during the walk and the services and she seemed all right, but as soon as we got back home she was frantic.

She insisted that all the black people who had seen her with us hated her for having a white family.

"They're going to come here and get us all!" she cried.

We tried to reassure her but she refused to be comforted. She was so terrified that we felt we must find someone who could calm her, and we made an urgent phone call to a Negro clergyman who was active in community affairs, and explained to him what had happened. He dropped everything and came to our house at once.

"Sure that's your mother," he told Shirley about me. "I can see that is your mother because she is the one who is taking care of you. Skin color doesn't make any difference. Nobody wants to take you away from your mother. Nobody, black or white."

He kept on explaining to her and comforting her. And somehow this tall, reassuring black man was able to project himself in Shirley's mind as a representative of the entire black race and give her their permission to be our child.

Both the black and white community supported our taking Shirley, and the young people's group at St. George's Church—which is one of the historic and more conservative old churches in Fredericksburg—contributed to her support.

It was not long after the abortive effort to have us evicted that one of our children, little David, developed appendicitis and needed surgery. I called upon the surgeon in our neighborhood who was uncomfortable having us for neighbors. It was he who performed the operation, and later treated other of our children. I hope that he found out, in visits with me and in getting to know the kids, that the reality of what was going on in our house was quite different from the rampant fantasies derived from gossip.

Whatever the reason, the whole movement eventually died down, and we stayed where we were.

By the end of the summer our household had increased by yet another child—our son Chucky had finished his special schooling on the West Coast and come back East to rejoin his family and re-enter public school. A graceful, beguiling boy, Chucky was coming home to a family quite different from the one he had left—and I was very much concerned about how he would react to the house full of brothers and sisters that we had assembled in his absence.

Fortunately for all of us, Chucky has an innate dash of savoir-faire. He seized up the family quickly, and solved the problem for us all by simply slipping into a place in the household, without fuss or commotion. The children all appeared glad to have this attractive new brother around and to our relief Chucky did not challenge anyone's position in the household. Nor did he seem distressed by the illness. Neither did he appear drawn to invest himself in the other children's well-being, as Tom did. I wondered if this was to be a permanent reaction on Chucky's part.

Of all the children, Dennis had seemed to be the most uneasy about Chucky's arrival. The healthier Dennis became, and his progress was fast, the more he considered himself as the "big brother" of the family. At this time, he and Tom had worked out a satisfactory relationship, with Tom's accepting Dennis as his elder brother. But apparently Dennis was very concerned that Chucky might challenge his status. To Dennis's great relief, Chucky did not appear interested in competing with Dennis for position of the senior child in the family, and Dennis seemed to relax into the unchallenged role of oldest son.

Until he hit me.

Chapter Eight

I DON'T EVEN REMEMBER what it was that Dennis and I were quarreling about. He had trailed me into our bedroom, and Moe was arbitrating while Dennis and I engaged in one of the interminable hassles which characterized our relationship at this time. I was sprawled on the bed, with Dennis sitting beside me. As he shouted something angry, I sat up suddenly, and before we realized what was happening he hit me and smashed my glasses.

Moe grabbed him, but it was unnecessary. Looking very young and confused, Dennis was saying to his father, "I didn't do anything! I didn't hit her!"

That, we found, was to prove typical of the several times during the next year when Dennis unexpectedly hit me. The pattern that emerged in these attacks was that when Dennis was angry about something and he and I would be arguing, be would perceive something which was not actually happening (in the above instance, he thought when I sat up suddenly that I was going to slap him) and that was his justification for his rage. After he had struck me, he could not remember that he had done so, and was confused and frightened. And he would not ac-

154

cept responsibility for the misperception that had triggered the event. He invariably justified it by saying such things as, "Well, she does a lot of stupid things," or "So how was I to know?"

As time went on I realized that at least one of the payoffs for Dennis of hitting me was how guilty and contrite Dennis became afterward. Similarly, when he had tried to hit me with the shovel, and I had comforted him, he wallowed in self-abasement. Even while persisting in describing me as the cause of what had happened, he would cling to me, beg forgiveness, assure me nothing like that would happen again, and plead with me not to reject him. For a while I gave in and comforted him, and protected him from Moe, accepting Dennis's accusations that I was doing something wrong or such things would not occur.

After a time, however, the seductive guilt wore thin. When Dennis was functioning well in every other way and still occasionally hitting me, it became obvious that he was not trying to work out the problem, and I stopped believing in his guilt and contrition. "If you cared about our relationship, you would work it out," I told him.

"Oh, I do care!" he would insist. "You can't give up on me. I need you so!"

And, feeling seduced and exploited, I would wait for the next time.

Meanwhile, in almost every other way Dennis was completely reliable and a great help to us all. Like Tom, he had a sensitivity to pathological behavior.

One of our headaches at this time, which was

a great worry to both Moe and me, was Elizabeth's insistence upon keeping up a relationship with her natural family. She continued to be quite attached to her parents, brother and sisters. One morning she came rushing in to find me, her eyes sparkling with excitement.

"Guess what!" She waved the letter under my nose. "My sister's getting married! And I'm going to the wedding!" Then, when I failed to respond to her enthusiasm, her voice faltered. "I can go, can't I, Mama? Please!"

"I don't think so," I said gently, stroking her hair back from her cheek. "You aren't ready for that kind of thing yet."

"Oh, but I don't want to miss it!" Elizabeth whimpered, her eyes swimming in tears. "Please, Mama, I do so want to go!"

I was feeling bad about depriving Elizabeth of something she seemed to want so much to do, when I received a call from her mother.

"We so want Elizabeth home for the wedding," she told me. "Surely you will let her come home for that. All her relatives will be expecting to see her. I promise we'll take the best care of her. And it will mean so much to us all—"

"But I don't think you understand," I began, realizing that by explaining I was already wavering. "Elizabeth is very sick. She needs constant watching."

"We can watch her here," her mother insisted. "We'll take ever such good care of her! It'll only be for the two days, and there certainly are enough of us to look after her—"

"Please, Mama, please!" Elizabeth was at my

side, jumping up and down in excitement. "I *do* want to go—"

"She must never be alone—" I warned.

"Oh, we wouldn't think of leaving her alone —" her mother reassured me.

"You must strip the bathroom and remove all the glasses and knives and anything that she could use to hurt herself—"

"I'll do that right now," she said. "Oh, it's so good of you, Mrs. Schiff. You do know what it means to us!"

I realized that I had given in, and hastily tried to recover the situation. "Suppose Dennis comes to the wedding," I suggested. "She could start the screaming thing, you know! He would recognize the signs and if he could stay close to her, and you could take care of her otherwise, it might work out."

"Oh, that's wonderful!"

"You do understand," I cautioned, "how careful you must be. She can become suicidal or homicidal any time she is upset."

"Of course." There was a note of laughter in her voice, as though my instructions were really too simple to be believed.

Her parents picked Elizabeth up and we arranged for Dennis to join them for the wedding. Again they assured me they could care for her, and no matter what Dennis's feelings about me were at the moment, this was the sort of situation he could be counted on to handle very well.

If there were trouble, I assumed it would be during the wedding itself. Later that night the telephone rang.

I was startled to hear Elizabeth's voice. "Mama, is that you?"

"Yes, Elizabeth. What's wrong?" I asked, my breath caught in my throat. I knew I should never have let her go.

"Well, I decided I better call you," Elizabeth said, her voice very upset, "because I'm alone in the house with the younger kids and I'm afraid I might kill my little sister."

"Where's your mother?" I demanded. "Where are your parents?"

"They went out to dinner and left me to baby-sit. But I'm scared—"

"When are they supposed to come home?" I asked her.

"In about an hour, I guess," Elizabeth said. "Mama, what shall I do?"

"You did the right thing to call me," I reassured her. "We'll think of something."

I knew Elizabeth would not act out if there were other people present. "How old is your brother?" I asked her. "Can you get him on the phone?"

I only vaguely remembered the boy—a lanky thirteen- or fourteen-year-old who could not begin to control Elizabeth if she became violent.

Fortunately, the youngster had already sized up the situation. "What shall I do?" he asked me.

"Take your little sister and go to a neighbor's at once," I told him. "Have some responsible grown-up, preferably a man, get back to your house so Elizabeth doesn't kill herself. Or if there isn't a man, have someone call the police.

Tell them she is suicidal. Now put Elizabeth back on the phone and I'll try to talk to her until help gets there."

While we talked to Elizabeth on the phone we sent someone out to call the police in the city where her family lived. (As a result of this crisis, we had a second phone installed in our house immediately afterward.) However, Elizabeth's brother had managed to do exactly as I said, and a few moments later a strange man came on the phone. I explained the problem to him, and he promised to stay until Elizabeth's parents arrived.

Later, her mother called me. "We were only gone for a little while," she said. "I don't know why Elizabeth was so upset!"

Furious, I realized that this woman would not understand a word I was saying! She refused to accept the fact that there had been any danger.

Elizabeth got through the wedding all right, but after she came home there were several furious, screaming episodes while she acted out her anger at her parents' neglect and unawareness of her needs. For the first time she began to have fantasies of killing them. Because her hold on reality was still so fragile, sometimes she believed that they were actually dead as a result of her "bad" thoughts.

"I killed them. I really did," she insisted one night. "All bashed and bloody. All of them. One by one I killed them all! Oh—I'm so bad! What'll happen to me? I should die, too!" Only a hasty late-at-night phone call to her family would convince Elizabeth that she was hallucinating, and that they were alive.

After that we began to take a stand against visits to the natural families, since it was apparent that a child could not be torn between two sets of parents and get well.

Reports of our success with the children had reached many of our therapist colleagues and they were developing a keen interest in what we were doing. They had begun thinking of patients they were treating in terms of our kind of therapy.

Shortly before Shirley came to live with us, the chief psychologist at one of the state hospitals, who knew me well, had suggested that we consider taking one of his patients, a boy who had a more serious history than the others we had thus far accepted. "If you two think you can cure schizos," he said, "I've got one for you, I *dare* you to try!"

Michael was only twenty-two years old but he had already spent nearly half his life in a psychiatric ward. His parents had divorced when he was an infant and his mother had to go to work to support herself and the child. While still an infant, Michael was shifted from baby-sitter to baby-sitter. Deprived of consistent care and mothering, he early developed into a disturbed child. When he began acting out his frustrations destructively, he was removed from his home and hospitalized at the age of twelve. Since then, he had learned, in the hospital through daily exposure to other patients, to be a lot sicker and a lot crazier than he actually was. Unfortunately, in most hospitals schizophrenics only get sicker.

When Moe first went to look at the boy, he reported that it was easy to see what the doctor had meant about him. After nine years' hospitalization, he was well on his way to becoming an adult vegetable. Too frightened of the other patients to run the risk of getting in their way, he spent most of his time sitting in a chair with his head hanging down between his knees.

I'm scared of the crazy ones, but they don't bother me if I don't look at them. Usually I just lie around all day and sleep, or stare at the walls or watch TV. A doctor comes by once a week and asks some questions but that's all the treatment there is. Sometimes I break cigarettes in half and smoke them all the way down until they burn my fingers real bad. Or I go to the lavatory and run the water till it gets boiling hot and fill the basin with it, and stick my hands in it and watch them turn red. Or I take razor blades and shave the hair off my legs, arms, and cut myself. It's something to do.

Tall, gaunt, white-faced, and with shaved red hair, Michael looked subhuman—like something out of a Frankenstein movie. He was being given more than fifty pills each day. Every time he got upset his medication was increased. Don Reed told us that if he didn't get the medication regularly he might die from withdrawal.

He had been taking nicotinic acid so long that his lips had turned brown and cracked. His tongue hung out of his mouth much of the time and his skin was scarred with one of the worst cases of acne I have seen. I had thought Dennis looked pretty awful. But Michael was really beyond belief. Also, he had a horrible smell. Besides the familiar schizophrenic smell, there was an odor from the untended sores and boils. He had simply not been kept clean in the hospital. Nor had he been given any regular form of exercise. His thin body was slack, without muscle tone or apparent strength.

Sometimes I get up and swing my arms around and maybe jump up and down for a while, and I make real bizarre faces with my mouth.

Michael was diagnosed catatonic. We did find out, however, that if we persisted in trying to get an answer from him, he would finally make some noncommittal reply, "I don't know about that," or "I'm confused."

He appeared extremely withdrawn. When we learned later how terrified he really was of many of the other patients, it did seem sensible that he should spend so much of his time with his head hanging down between his knees. It was a very good position for not seeing anything that was coming at him.

I don't talk to the others because I'm scared of them. I talk to myself instead.

When they asked me if I want to go home with them I said yes but I'm scared of that, too. I've been in the hospital so long that the idea of leaving frightens me. At least, here I know what it's like. . . .

When we did take him home with us, our dear friend Don Reed blew up. "Oh, this one is really too much!" he protested. "Do you think you can perform miracles?"

We weren't sure how we could handle him. For several weeks we let him sit around our house with his head down, burning himself with cigarettes, just as he had done in the hospital.

Then we decided we had had enough of that. What was the point in allowing Michael to remain so withdrawn when he could be learning to communicate? We began to wage all-out war on his withdrawal.

"We aren't going to put up with this any more," Moe told Michael. "You must move around. You must answer when you are spoken to. If I see you sitting with your head hanging down, I'm going to spank you."

Michael looked up at Moe with the first expression of interest we had seen from him.

He did not reply. But he stopped sitting around with his head down. The next time Moe found Michael burning himself with his cigarette, he did spank him. Michael stopped burning himself.

At first Michael was too weak to do chores or engage in much physical activity. But gradually he began to regain his strength. Dr. Reed took him off his heavy medication by degrees, until eventually he had nothing but nighttime medication. We use medication when it is absolutely needed to calm a child who is having a psychotic episode, but we often find better ways to work things out. Tranquilizers, upon which hospitals rely, are kept to a minimum so that the child is alert and his pathology can be dealt with directly.

The worst thing that had happened to Michael during his long hospitalization was that he had lost all motivation to get well. It took constant goading by Moe and me and the other children before he finally decided that he would like to rejoin the human race. When he did begin to relate to other people, Michael discovered a whole side of his nature that he did not even know existed. He learned that he liked to help other people. He liked being needed.

After he had been with us about eight months and had begun to get better, I asked him if he would like to see a dermatologist about his skin. As he had begun to relate to others, Michael was taking more interest in his own appearance, and he was pleased to go to the doctor and begin treatments. With his skin being cared for, his naturally curly red hair grown out, and a few pounds of weight added, we were all pleased to discover that our "subhuman" hospital patient was emerging as a good-looking boy.

Seeing the pitiful condition that Michael was in when we took him made me bitter about hospital care. There is no reason to keep a child sitting for ten years. There is nothing to be gained from an environment like that. Patients exist in that dim world only because their families cannot cope with them and there is nowhere else for them to go. The hospital, in this sense, is primarily custodial, offering a patient protection, but no chance to recover.

In one hospital I visited, and they are supposed to have a good children's unit, there is a room where they put all the children who smear feces. Each day the children are put in the barren room in their underpants, where they can spend their time dirtying themselves, one another, and the walls. At meal time they are taken out, showered, and fed, and then returned to their pen.

When I first saw this, I asked one of the staff, "Why?"

"They all smear feces so we decided to put them together where they can go ahead and do it."

It was my impression that the children spent their days like that, with no treatment and no attention. When I asked what the justification was for such care, I was told that they were too hard to care for otherwise.

But just how much feces can a child produce in one day? It seemed to me that if they were cleaned when it happened then they could have done something more constructive all day long than stand around in their own manure like penned animals.

The alternative would have been to toilet train the children. It is not that hard to do, even with a regressed schizophrenic. But I doubt anyone has explained that to the nurse who would be responsible for the training.

In most state hospitals there simply aren't enough therapists to treat patients. Even when a patient is seen regularly, therapists are seldom willing to offer the kind of care the patient wants and needs. Our daughter Barbara, when she was a day patient at a hospital and saw a doctor regularly, pleaded with her doctor to mother her, but the doctor refused, telling Barbara that she had a "pathological need for love." When Barbara was able at long last to get in touch with her feelings and cry, for the first time, a nurse told her to "shut up."

Some hospitals claim success with shock treatment of schizophrenics. Our daughter Bunny, who had a great deal of shock, describes it this way:

That dreadful machine. The poor helped, helpless people. I cannot stand to see or know the devastation and the people who say, "yes, it helped," because they cannot stand the thought that all they went through was for nothing. . . .

So far as our experience goes, shock treatment is apt to be a tragic mistake. The physiological effects can be brain damage, loss of memory, mental confusion. Psychologically, shock is apt to fixate a patient at whatever age level he was in his regression. Schizophrenics may appear to behave better after shock treatment for the same reason that a small child is quiet immediately after he has been severely punished: They have literally been frightened into acceptable behavior. But they are no less sick. The pathology is simply hidden and when the patient is exposed to stress, he will crack up again.

Bunny had more experience with hospitalization than any of our children except Michael. I began seeing her while she was still a hospital patient, following a suicide attempt.

No sleep possible. Fear beyond any I have

*ever known. Nothing is big enough, strong
enough, to hide me. I feel like I am plunging. . . .*

Her husband had learned about TA from
Bunny's brother who was living on the West
Coast, and he had contacted me as the TA
therapist closest to Bunny, and asked me to see
her. The doctor who was treating Bunny at the
time wrote me a letter warning me that she was
not worth my time—nor anyone else's. This was
one of many hospitalizations and she had never
responded to treatment. Apparently the doctor
felt that she was taking up valuable time and
bedspace that might more profitably be given
to someone else, since it seemed inevitable that
she would eventually succeed in killing herself.
The hospital did agree to keep her for a few
weeks if I would see her as an outpatient.

Her husband drove her from the hospital to
see me.

She was a slight, girlish-looking young woman
with a mass of black hair framing her pale face.
Her body was strangely misshapen under a
loose, flowing dress which covered her arms to
the wrists and fell to the floor. Her face was
round and very white. Delicate veins showed
through the skin of her fragile-looking hands.

My first interview with Bunny involved no
coherent conversation at all. She talked in confused, garbled symbols, and I attempted to in-
terpret them, understand some of what she was
saying: birds, cows, moons, fences.

She spoke to me with her eyes—they sent out
desperate messages of sickness past coping,
despair, and constant fear. Even fear of me. Her

mouth, pouting and angry, told me something else: How bitter she was toward everyone and everything, how everyone had failed her, that trying to kill herself might well be an ugly, angry game. I had better be careful, I thought to myself, as I discovered how angry she was with therapists. She could kill herself to spite me.

What can it be that I am so very much afraid of? I want to scream and at times I think I'll just snap in two.

What hurts me so? Why must I die? Yet my dilemma can only be resolved by my death. I don't understand how we survive—how life goes on and time goes by while each one of us is impaled upon some pain or despair....

Oh, please let some good come of this meeting. I wonder what she thinks of me? Is she contemptuous like the doctors who have seen too much of me already?

I try not to hope. But I do want to be worth my days. Once I had a glimpse and I need that glimpse as a photograph to help me to find and recognize a missing person—a Bunny to live this life I have left hanging about me....

Till now, the girls that I had dealt with were chronologically young—fifteen to twenty-two. Despite her fragile child look, Bunny was a good deal older. She had been married for several years—probably the one healthy, independent act she had performed, although the marriage in itself could not stop or sustain the enormity of her illness.

She had been sick, so far as hospital records showed, since she was eleven years old and began to have colitis. Neither psychotherapy nor other medical care had helped. At twenty-one she had had her colon removed. Ileostomy is a rare operation for one so young but apparently the colitis progressed along with the symptoms of schizophrenia, until her doctors felt there was no choice, and the operation was performed, leaving Bunny permanently handicapped. In addition to the surgery, at some point she was given a great deal of cortisone which resulted in many side effects, including the painful arthritis which has been a constant problem since I have known her.

Unable to cope with her sickness, Bunny's father and mother had reacted to it with anger so that Bunny, early on, got the message that her life was valueless. She had a suicide script from both of her parents, and, as a result, had been determinedly seeking her own death for years. That she had not succeeded was just one of those odd quirks of fate—where someone always managed to get her to medical aid before her last breath. Judging by her hospital record— ileostomy, cardiac collapse, drug abuse, alcoholism, slashed veins—she was near death innumerable times.

After my first interview with Bunny I knew that I would manage somehow to treat her. I liked and trusted her husband, John Christy. A slender, serious, bearded young man, he was clearly devoted to his wife and I knew I could count on him to support whatever care we would give her. Until now, he was obviously the one person who believed that Bunny could live and get well. Now there were two of us.

"If you consider taking this patient," warned the psychiatrist most recently assigned to treat Bunny, "you're as crazy as she is!"

Chapter Nine

BECAUSE OF BUNNY'S AGE, physical condition, and the added complication of her marriage, I did not at first consider reparenting her as we were doing with the other children.

When I began to see her, the tentative plan was that I would see her only in my private practice. However, within days after Bunny was discharged from the hospital she made still another suicide attempt, with an overdose of drugs, and landed in the intensive care unit at the Medical College for Virginia. It was obvious that if I was going to do anything for her, it would have to be on a more sustained basis than outpatient treatment.

The psychiatrist who saw her at the hospital recommended that for Bunny's own protection John commit her to a state hospital. John refused. Instead, he came to me to discuss what plans we could make for her daily treatment with me.

I found myself reacting as much to John's confidence in me as to Bunny's situation. There was something very compelling and appealing in this quiet young man's need for his wife to get well, and his belief in my ability to cure her.

Usually in a marriage in which one partner is

sick, the marriage itself is suspect, since the spouse often has some investment in his partner's pathology. As most other therapists, I had learned to regard a marriage as apt to be detrimental to attempts at treatment. This pattern seemed especially likely in a marriage like Bunny's and John's where the pathology was well established before the marriage took place.

I was puzzled both by John's apparent sincerity about his desire for his wife to get well, and in the confidence he inspired in me. I explained some of this to him, then asked him, directly:

"Why did you marry a woman who was so sick?"

"I really don't know," he admitted. Then he looked straight at me. "But if you think it's important, I'll come into treatment, too, and we'll find out. Believe me, I'll do whatever is necessary for Bunny to get well."

I believe him. And it was enough, for now, that he would cooperate with me. Later, we were to find out more about his reasons for marrying Bunny. At the moment I was satisfied that he did want to see her get well.

We discussed how I might treat Bunny as a day patient at the house, so that she would be under our care during the time he was at his job. John was a reporter on a newspaper in Richmond. He worked long and unusual hours but he was willing to move to Fredericksburg to be close to us, and then commute the hundred miles each day if I would consider taking Bunny into day care.

I spelled out to John precisely what his role

must be to support our treatment, and insure that there would be no repeating the latest suicide attempt that had catapulted Bunny back into the hospital. I told him that he would be expected to participate in Bunny's treatment. We would depend on him to be protective in regard to her suicidal impulses. He would be required to relate to the entire family.

"You are going to have to adapt yourself to unusual physical and emotional demands," I warned him. "It will be an exhausting experience for you. And I can't tell you when it will end. Do you think you can do it?"

"I can do it," John assured me. "I can do anything that will keep her from being committed."

John located a small apartment in Fredericksburg and moved Bunny there directly from the hospital. Each morning at seven he brought Bunny to our house and left her napping on the couch in the living room with one of the children to watch her. Some time between supper and one or two A.M. he reappeared. If he were early he spent the evening with us. Then he and Bunny would go home for the night.

Bunny was physically debilitated at the time she came to us, so the course of her treatment was modified by her physical illness. Generally I have found that those patients with the most physical strength get well fastest. But the opposite was true with Bunny, who, despite constant pain and frustration from her ileostomy, arthritis, and pneumonia, worked steadily and productively in treatment.

The first hurdle we had to surmount with Bunny was to convince her that her life *was* worthwhile.

She had every reason to doubt it. Throughout the course of her illness her parents, and later, therapists had reinforced Bunny's negative self-concept.

Once I cut my wrists when my parents were away for the weekend. I tried to keep the cuts bleeding but I didn't die. When they came home and found me in the hospital they were furious. My father told me I would be accused of attempted murder and that I was in real trouble.

Bunny's hospital experiences had only served to reinforce the suicide script she had from her parents. Her memory of hospitals is doctors and nurses standing over her bed saying angry things to her. It is not unusual for hospital personnel, dismayed at the responsibility of caring for a patient who may kill herself any moment, to let the patient know they consider him a nuisance. Bunny overheard one nurse say, "Well, in her situation, I'd kill myself, too." A psychiatrist remarked to her and John, in reference to the pain Bunny was experiencing, that he considered the idea of killing herself was one of the healthiest reactions Bunny had demonstrated. In several instances, the means of self-destruction were made available to Bunny by well-meaning advocates of euthanasia.

We put Bunny on suicide supervision so that she was never out of someone's sight in her hours with us. We also made a concerted effort to see to it that nothing was said to or about her that would, like the suicide messages from the past, give her permission to hurt or kill herself. At that, it was over a year before her impulses toward self-destruction began to significantly decrease.

When Bunny first came to us, I was concerned about what Moe's reaction to her would be. He is uncomfortable around handicapped people. But shortly after Bunny's arrival, before she was even coherent in her contacts with me, a relationship of great warmth and depth began to develop spontaneously between father and daughter.

I sleep late in the mornings, since I am usually up most of the night, and I do not get up when Moe leaves for the office in the morning. While I slept it became part of Moe's morning ritual to greet Bunny and check on how she was that day. Usually he found her dozing on the sofa in the living room. If the air was chilly, he pulled the blanket up over her shoulders before he kissed her good-bye.

Often I found her there, still napping, when I got up, a faint smile on her face from his morning kiss.

No one ever complained about having to care for Bunny. Often suicidal patients are negativistic and unpleasant, but even when she was sickest Bunny managed to contribute a great deal to everyone around her. All her anger was directed at herself.

As Bunny became a part of the family, we all also grew closer to her bearded, soft-spoken husband, John. His original commitment to Bunny's getting well did not falter. There was not a single instance when John did not do exactly what we asked of him for his wife's welfare. Even so, I knew I dared not be comfortable with the situation until I knew for sure that John's relationship with Bunny was not in any way predicated on Bunny's being physically or mentally ill.

It was impossible to approach Bunny herself about her relationship with John. Her natural parents had told her that no man would ever want a "mutilated woman" and she was desperately afraid that John would ultimately reject her. We therefore had to depend entirely on him to report on any problems that arose between them. As Bunny improved John became aware of his own need for treatment.

While I never considered John as seriously disturbed, I do not believe Bunny could have gotten well without the shared experience of working through their separate and mutual problems. I grew more and more impressed with John's integrity and courage as he willingly exposed and confronted the traumas of his own childhood: the fright and confusion he had experienced as a boy centered around his own father's illness with epilepsy, his incapacitation and eventual death. That John had not been able to care for his father had contributed to his motivation in marrying someone sick whom he could prove that he could care for. It was when Bunny began to get well that his own problems surfaced. Fortunately for them both, John had the courage to face—and understand—his problems, so he could become free to make normal, healthy demands on his wife. His feelings for Bunny did not depend on her remaining sick.

Later, when she was able to talk about their relationship, Bunny referred to her marriage as "the one healthy thing I did." The period immediately following the marriage had been the most productive part of her life. She had been able to function better than ever before, probably because of the separation from her mother. However, when the young couple was forced to share a household with John's mother, Bunny's newfound strength began to collapse. Without quite knowing why, she became increasingly confused and incapable of functioning. She began drinking in an attempt to cope. Soon the drinking was out of hand.

It gallops out of the bottle when I'm tired, nervous or scared. I hope and pray someone will knock on our door and save me but no one comes. I want to be worth something more than anyone will ever know. Please, somebody, come!

When they sought help from a therapist, they were advised to live apart from the mother-in-law, but were in no position financially to do so. Bunny rapidly went downhill. It was typical of her penchant for clear symbolism that she slashed her wrists the night before Mother's Day.

The major problem in Bunny's relationship with me derived from the symbiotic attachment she had with her natural mother.

Symbiosis is a normal part of infancy. A baby believes his mother shares his feelings and re-

sponds to her feelings with total involvement.
By the time the child is two, he understands
that he and his mother are separate. But if his
infant needs were neglected, he may spend his
life trying to get the needs met by controlling
mothering in some way. A symbiotic relationship
involves the attempted "merging" of individuals:
Two or more people seem to divide up the func-
tions of a single personality. Thus, only one of
them can get angry, drive a car, or read a book.
They have a secret contract never to compete so
there can never be dissention.

It is apt to occur, as in both Bunny's and our
daughter Barbara's case when, denied the normal expression of love from a mother, a child
tries frantically to cling to the parent in an
unhealthy way, and become part of her.

When Barbara was first in the house, I developed an aversion to her, without knowing
quite why, which left me feeling guilty and
frightened. Fearing that it was something within
me, I avoided discussing it with her until our
relationship became seriously disrupted and the
problem had to be confronted. Then I told Barbara, in a group, that I kept having fantasies
that she wanted to eat me.

"That's right," Barbara said promptly.

We were all startled.

"But how?" someone asked her.

Barbara looked puzzled. Then, after a moment's hesitation, she said, "With my teeth."

Bunny did not have fantasies about eating me
but she was seriously afraid of developing a symbiosis with me, such as she had had with her

own mother. "You're the mother now," she told me. "I'm afraid of getting into that again."

"I don't believe that could happen without my having some part in it," I told her confidently, feeling really sure of no lurking desire on my part for any such relationship. However, my assurance turned out to be ill-founded. As time went on we were confronted with such manifestations of the disturbance as Bunny's having menstrual periods only when I was away from home.

Bunny's experiences with her father (whom she considered to be loving, but sadistic) had not been good either; but they were less frightening than those with her mother, and it was therefore easier for her to relate at first to Moe than to me.

Although Bunny was already an established artist in our area, she said little about her work. With her very low self-esteem she defined herself as "a person who draws." As she regained strength, I encouraged her to utilize more of her energy for her drawing. Her work contributed toward her getting well. And it was an interest which she and Moe shared. Music was another shared interest that deepened and strengthened the bond between them.

Bunny and I often talked about what it would be like to get well. It was apparent that she perceived health as being able to withstand or cope with a terrible world, meeting the demands of other people in order to prove her value. I tried to tell her about a different kind of world, where people loved and laughed and played together, but for a long, long time the conversations ended with Bunny's affirming, with desperate sincerity, that when she was well, then she would be worthwhile.

Bunny's childhood colitis, which had necessitated the eventual surgery, was, I knew, a symptom of the deep anal anger Bunny had experienced toward her mother, who had failed to provide the unconditional love infants need to be healthy. Because of her confusion about having to meet other people's needs rather than having her own met, we established no expectation of Bunny except that she allow herself to be loved and cared for.

Since symbols are so important to the schizophrenic, I am always alert for ways to support a child's feeling noticed, loved, recognized as an individual. Often that means going to the trouble to find a particular gift—like Eric's four-foot blue teddy bear and Shirley's giant peppermint lollipops. Bunny rarely asked for anything, but once she timidly told me she needed winter gloves.

I was expecting mittens or plain wool gloves but Mom shopped and shopped and finally found me these beautiful leather, fur-lined gloves. I am amazed that she would take so much trouble to find the perfect thing for me—when "things" mean so little to her. It is an important statement to me—a symbol that she wants to take care of me.

It was hard for us to understand how Bunny had elicited such pessimistic reactions from other therapists. Even in the beginning it was apparent that behind all the sickness and anger was a very special person, deeply artistic, spiritual, touched with mystery. She attracted people to her easily, and was sensitive and responsive to those around her. She had not been with us long when someone noticed that Elizabeth's "holding stone" had been decorated with flowers.

"How did you ever get it away from her?" we asked Bunny.

"I asked her if she would like to see a flower come to life," Bunny answered with her shy, little-girl smile.

Elizabeth, at this time, was suddenly getting much better, much to our confusion. Whereas Dennis's progress had shown a certain continuity—we had known fairly well what stage he was in, and when he progressed to the next—Elizabeth had suddenly developed a strong functional new Parent incorporated from us, and most of her craziness promptly subsided. She seemed to be skipping all the in-between development and taking a giant leap from irrational to rational behavior.

Shortly after Elizabeth developed her Parent, her thinking cleared up. Delusions seemed to drop away, she gave up her bizarre postures, her suicidal script, and also much of her little-girl naïveté. She began talking about leaving home, going back to school. Delighted as we were with the remarkable change in our lovely little daughter, the transformation seemed too fast, too easy. While we could not pinpoint anything specific, Moe and I both hedged about letting her make plans to leave home.

Elizabeth reacted to our hesitation with obvious fright. "Don't you believe I'm getting well?" she demanded. "What's the matter?"

"Of course you're getting well," I assured her. "It's just that until so recently you were a pretty sick little girl."

"But I'm almost well," she insisted. "Oh, I feel so different! I want to do so many things!"

By Christmas she had made such remarkable progress that we allowed her to make plans to enter college for the spring semester in February. Before she left the house Elizabeth presented her "holding stone" to one of the other girls who was sicker than she was.

As Elizabeth suddenly spiraled toward success, Rosita's condition deteriorated to a point where there was no advantage to our continuing our efforts at working with her. She was no longer responding to our care and there was apparently nothing we could do to avert the downhill course.

We gave up on Rosita. This failure gave me one of my lowest moments. I cannot help but feel that it was I who failed with her. And yet I do not understand how or why. She should have gotten well. She had made such a lot of progress in the beginning—only to lose it.

The Child in me believes there is some kind of magic in loving—that if I had only loved Rosita enough, I could have found a way to help her get well. Sometimes I could feel the wish for health and happiness—only to have it slip out of both our grasps.

Tom, who loved Rosita, says, "It was more

important for her to play games and manipulate people than it was for her to get well." But I don't really believe that. For me the experience parallels that of my losing the first little Vikki who died so mysteriously in her crib. It seems that there is something I should have known or noticed or thought about. As we learned more about "split personalities" from the hebephrenic youngsters I often wondered. "If we had only known those things in the beginning. . . ."

John, Rosita's natural brother, remained with us. The two children were so alike in many ways, and yet so opposite. John so big, Rosita so small. John, sheltering and defending his anger, Rosita so subject to stubborn outbursts. Slowly but consistently, John got better. When he finally left home it was with a good job, plans to marry and return to school. John's was our first wedding and we could not have been prouder of any son.

But why was it, I wondered over and over again, that I could be John's mother and not Rosita's?

It is a question I have never been able to answer.

Chapter Ten

SHIRLEY WAS NOT LOOKING any better at this time, either. Although we no longer had to haul her off to the hospital daily because of our new access to medication, caring for her continued to be a terrible strain on the entire family. Month followed month with no sign of improvement. Constantly hassling with her taxed us all, especially Dennis who assumed a lot of responsibility for her. Since she was still not relating well to him, Moe left her pretty much alone.

Sometimes it looked to me as though Shirley was deliberately refusing to get well. She was getting her needs met and getting herself taken care of and it was as though she was getting even for all the years when no one took care of her. She was also getting even with us for being white and "pretending" to love her. She denied that our love could be real. "I'm not your baby!" she screamed at me, over and over again. "Don't you try to tell me I am. I'm not. I'm different from the others. Can't you see?"

Jacqui, I don't need you to say good-night to me any more nor do I need you to tell me that you love me. I already know the score quite well. I know that I could never be the kind of woman you would want me to be and you know it. Quit kidding yourself. It's not your fault. It's mine that I would engage in such behavior that your love becomes disgust and exasperation. Instead of being a joy to be with I am the opposite. I'm not fun to be around. Just a pain in the ass. I am not like one of the other kids here and they know it. I'm not like Elizabeth or Irene. Am I? No, I am not. Don't try to tell me I am. Admit that I am hopeless and give up on me before it is too late. . . .

I knew that Shirley knew viscerally, just as I did, that I loved her. Yet intellectually she could not accept it. She pretended to hate me. She ranted and screamed at me, provoked me constantly, trying to prove to us both that I was an inadequate mother. Yet when she was violent and trying to hurt other people she saw to it that she did not injure me. Whenever I was engaged in the struggle it was markedly reduced so there was no chance of even accidental injury.

She was screaming at me in the kitchen one day when I was cutting bread with a long, sharp knife.

"You just let me get my hands on that knife and I'll stab you with it!" she raged.

I turned to her, so that we were face to face and silently handed her the knife.

She stared at it in horror, backed away from me, then dropped to the floor, dissolved into howling, infant tears.

"You see?" I said, comforting her in my arms. "You don't need to be afraid of killing me."

I knew the danger was far greater that Shirley might succeed in killing herself.

I hate myself. I hate you. I want to kill . . . I am so afraid. I want to go away. Let me go away. . . .

It was hard for me to accept the fact that despite my love for her, despite the constant care I gave her, Shirley still wanted to die. Once, after reenacting her parents' fight scene she hacked her arm horribly so that it would look like her mother's arm had looked that terrible night. At other times she showed her desire to die by refusing to eat, so that it was necessary for me to force-feed her for days at a time.

One afternoon when I had left Dennis in charge of the house for a few hours, I drove home to find him waiting agitatedly for me out in the driveway.

"Shirley swallowed a whole bottleful of aspirin," he told me. "I called the rescue squad and they have taken her to the hospital."

When Moe and I arrived at the hospital, Shirley was in convulsions. When I entered the room she tried frantically to turn away from me, to deny that I was there.

Moe and I stood over her, clinging helplessly to one another, watching this child we loved and had tried to care for, drawing up in what appeared to be death throes.

I reached out to her, and tried to talk to her, to persuade her that there was something to live for.

Shirley shook her head frantically from side to side on the white sheet, her plump brown face ashen and pinched with agony. "I love you," she choked, her voice a thin thread of pain. "I love you. But I want to die. Please go away and let me die!"

"You can't die, Shirley. I won't let you die." I leaned over her bed so that she could not escape my face or my words. "You must live, Shirley. We love you and we want you to live. You are our daughter, Shirley. You can't deny that. You have your life ahead of you. You haven't even begun to live yet. You can't quit now. You must keep on living, Shirley, even though it hurts you. You hate yourself. We don't hate you. We love you. You are a good girl. A beautiful girl. You must live. . . ."

I did not know what—if anything—would reach her now. I just kept on talking, saying what was in my heart, and forcing her to acknowledge my presence, to accept that I was there and to know that she was not free to slip away from me.

Moe says I talked Shirley into staying alive. I don't know what happened. Whatever it was, her convulsions finally subsided and Shirley lived.

I have tried to escape from you, not because I wanted to but because my sickness wanted me to. I have tried to sink inside myself and never return. I tried pushing you far away but you would not be pushed. You touched me. You stroked my face, my arm, my hand. I was a silent resister but I could not resist long. Suddenly I felt life and warmth again. I was no longer dead, tight, cold and withdrawn into my-

188 : ALL MY CHILDREN

self. You had won, for you showed that love has
more power than sickness. You gave me your
love and for that I RETURNED!

Yet when we brought her home Shirley
showed no greater investment in getting well.
Day followed day with more failures, more dis-
appointments. Little sign of progress. Even her
self-styled champion, Dennis, finally had had
enough.

"You're spoiling Shirley," he charged me.
"You are overprotecting her. She is not working
to get well. She is not trying. All the kids know
it. You know it."

For the other children this was the cardinal
sin. They could accept anything from one another—except the failure to try to get well.

I had been shielding Shirley, I knew. If I had
a favorite child, I suppose the kids would all say
it was Shirley.

"You indulge her," Dennis accused me. "You
let her take advantage of the fact that she is
your favorite. And it isn't as though you were
indulging her because it's to *her* best interests.
It's because of your own investment in her. I
think you owe it to her as well as the rest of us
to confront her with what she's doing and make
her stop it. She's never going to get well if you
let her keep on this way."

I knew Dennis was right. He wasn't baiting
me for any secret motives of his own. Shirley did
have an enormous amount of pathology to con-
tend with, and layered on top of that was the
problem of race. But I realized that I had been
indulgent for too long. If another child had

shown as little interest in getting well as Shirley had, and been as hard to care for, we would have given up long before this.

I tried to think of a way to confront Shirley, but was unable to find a starting place until the next time I was furiously angry at her. Then I was able to do what I needed to do.

"I'm sick and tired of the way you've been acting and so is everyone else!" I told her. "No one else gets away with this kind of behavior and you aren't going to get away with it any longer either! Now you either make a decision to be our child and get well, accept the things we are trying to give you, or you can go back to your natural family!"

Shirley had been listening with an expression of sullen anger. But as I said "back to your natural family" her face tensed into momentary fright. Death did not frighten Shirley, but rejection did. The possibility of being returned alive to the world from which she had come to us was unthinkable.

"I'll kill myself," she threatened.

"That's up to you!" I told her.

Shirley turned angrily from me and stormed out of the room.

I followed her to the door of the girls' bedroom. She opened the closet, yanked out a suitcase and started packing. "Dennis will take you back to Charlottesville when you're ready," I said. I turned and went back to my own room.

By suppertime Shirley had not left the house. She packed her suitcase, then sat around sulking, avoiding me and everyone else. At dinner she sat silent, her face a battleground of hate and despair. She would not speak to any of us and when Elizabeth reached out to her and tried to touch her, Shirley struck angrily at her hand.

The next morning Shirley was still with us. But she was sullen, withdrawn and non-communicative. It was not until that night, when we had all gathered around the living room for a family group that she finally spoke.

She looked around the circle of faces, obviously still warring with herself, her eyes avoiding mine, chewing her lips with her sharp, white teeth.

"I don't want to leave," she said in a low voice.

"If you stay you will have to work," I said to her. "You will have to show us that you want to get well."

"I will," she said, her head down, still not meeting my eyes. "I promise to try harder."

It was enough to win her a reprieve.

There then began a subtle change in Shirley. She continued to be negativistic and difficult to get along with, but her behavior was less overtly pathological. She stopped trying to kill or maim herself. She assumed more responsibility at home, and she began showing more interest in forming relationships outside the family. It was apparent that while Shirley's relationship with me was the one in which she was most deeply involved, it was also the one most likely to trigger the pathology.

When Shirley graduated from high school in the spring of 1968, we agreed with her that in spite of the enormous amount of pathology re-

maining, it might be good for her to separate
from me, to try to establish herself in an environment where she would be forced to meet
healthy expectations. Shirley was accepted in a
small college about seventy-five miles from home
and we decided that her motivation around
academic achievement, which seemed remarkably high, might be the key to her moving
ahead. So we began to plan for Shirley to go
away to college.

Chapter Eleven

As our second year merged into the third, and the first children to have been reparented moved out into the world, we watched for signs of instability in their new personality structures. Elizabeth and Mark were in Charlottesville attending school, and Dennis was planning to join them in the fall.

Our first group of children were growing up— but always there were new babies. For every child who left home, there seemed to be three more ready to replace him. I was learning to hate the ring of the telephone; to dread reading the day's mail. I had not yet found ways to defend myself against the children who needed so much and appealed so desperately.

I had a dream. In the dream I was attending a professional meeting. While a party was in progress in my room, I went into the bathroom and got into the tub. Then, suddenly, with the tub full of water, I began to have babies. First a robust boy whom I knew to be Mark. Then a baby girl, Irene. Finally, a very skinny baby, much littler than the first two, with a shock of frizzy hair—undoubtedly our latest child Geoff. Frantically I juggled the three infants to try to keep them above water. I thought about calling out to the people in the next room—wondered how they would react—and awoke.

We *were* juggling a great many children in what was, legally at least, a rather haphazard way. Moe and I were afraid that if we became "properly organized," the autonomy of the family might be sacrificed. But after much planning and consultation, the Schiff Rehabilitation Project finally emerged and was legalized. Now we began thinking in terms of training other people in the work we were doing and perhaps opening other homes like ours to reach more of the youngsters who were constantly reaching out to us.

We had hopes that some of our children would want to follow us into this work. Dennis already displayed as much knowledge of schizophrenia as most professional therapists. John Christy had proved to be an able assistant when we called upon him. Bunny mentioned wanting to train to become a therapist after she got well.

Bunny had come to us in the autumn of 1967. By the following spring, the improvement in her was readily apparent. By summer, health was becoming a reality.

As for Dennis, although he seemed fine in almost all other ways, his game with me continued. No amount of pushing seemed to motivate his working it through. Repressed anger can be aired and then it dissipates, but anal and infant anger, which comes from the feelings of the preverbal Child, has to be exposed and then relinquished. And Dennis continued to be unwilling or unable to do this.

The problem affected Dennis's relationships with the rest of the family also. The other children were indignant and frightened at the possibility of Dennis's seriously hurting me. Moe felt torn between his concern for the youngster who now seemed so securely our oldest son, and his fears for my safety.

Until that summer the incidents had always been between Dennis and me, not involving others. They usually involved Dennis's hitting me, followed by confusion and contrition. But as Moe put more pressure on Dennis to solve the problem, the pattern shifted.

Dennis often had difficulty asking for things he wanted—to borrow money—a car—time off. Typically he would tell me the problem and wait for me to make a suggestion. For example, "I'd like to see a movie in Washington," and I would respond, "Well, you could take the car Friday night."

So I noted that it was unusual when, one afternoon, Dennis said, "Would you mind if I took Saturday off?"

I said I didn't know of any reason that would not be okay, and was pleased at Dennis's showing more initiative. However, when I later mentioned to Moe that Dennis would not be home Saturday, he said "But Dennis promised to do something for me on Saturday."

When Moe confronted Dennis with this, Dennis responded defensively. "It wasn't my idea. Mom said I should go!"

"I did not!" I said, furious at his trying to shift blame.

"You're a goddam liar!" Dennis snarled at me. Moe slapped him.

Dennis backed against the sink. "You keep your fucking hands off me!" he yelled. "You touch me again and I'll knock you on your ass."

Moe slapped him again.

For a moment they locked in struggle, but then Moe went down hard, striking his head on the oven door as he fell. Dennis moved back to kick him, and I jumped in, locking my arms around Dennis's neck and clinging frantically to him. Dennis struck me several times before he broke my hold and then I fell between them.

At that moment some of the boys got to us and tackled Dennis. He put up very little struggle, obviously glad to quit. But he was still furiously angry.

Moe was clinging to the sink, swaying dizzily, and I knew he was hurt.

"You get out of this house and never come back!" Moe yelled angrily.

Dennis didn't answer. He stood looking from one to another of us, then shook the boys off and walked away. Several of the youngsters followed him.

I knew at once that Moe was sorry about what he had said. As one of the boys and I helped him into the car, to go to the hospital emergency room, he said to me, "I didn't mean that."

"I'll talk to him," I said.

I went to the boys' room where a miserable cluster of children were watching Dennis pack. "Do you want to talk to me?" I asked. He was still angry, but he nodded, and his lips were white and trembling.

I went carefully over the whole incident with him. For the first time he was aware of the violence and remembered what he had done. We went back over the original transaction about his asking for the day off, and he sat down on the bed, shaking and confused.

"Did I hurt him?" he asked. "Is he hurt bad?"

Moe had suffered a slight concussion. But it did not require hospitalization, and by the time he returned home, with instructions for twenty-four hours' bedrest, his anger at Dennis had evaporated. He was relieved that Dennis was in touch with what had happened and more than willing to accept an apology.

Dennis did not go into his contrite game this time. He seemed sincerely ashamed and sorry about hurting his father, and he did not look for any payoffs in terms of forgiveness and reassurance from me or from his father.

He did not apologize for hurting me, or in any way indicate that he thought he owed me an apology. Both he and Moe made it clear that they felt I had had no right to jump into the middle of their fight. When Moe did make Dennis apologize for swearing at me, he did so sullenly, managing to communicate clearly that he felt no real regret.

There was still something very wrong between Dennis and me.

The fight between Moe and Dennis left me puzzling over the pieces of what seemed to be developing into an insoluble mystery. The pat-

tern of previous angry episodes with me, in which
he provoked fights in order to be contrite afterward, and pick up free strokes was clear to me.
But his game continued even though it wasn't
working any more. I could not understand why
he was so indifferent to my feelings while at the
same time clinging to me and insisting that he
needed me. Why, also, had he seemed so ready
to accept responsibility for the quarrel with Moe,
and yet been unwilling to recognize any responsibility in the game with me?

I was hopeful that when Dennis left home to
return to school his motivation to continue the
game would decline. He went back to the University of Virginia as a full-time student in September 1968, and he and Mark and another student arranged to share an apartment in Charlottesville. They celebrated their move with a
housewarming party to which they invited
several of their younger brothers and sisters from
home.

Ordinarily, Moe and I would not have let the
younger children go that distance to a party, but
we felt confident that they would be safe with
Mark and Dennis.

Later, we learned marijuana had been used at
the party. The drugs did not belong to either
Mark or Dennis. They had been brought by a
guest. But Dennis had known that the marijuana
was there and had done nothing about it.

I was furious. One of our younger boys who
attended the party had an extensive history of
drug use and his psychosis had been precipitated
by drugs. Dennis knew how dangerous it was for

him to be exposed to drugs, and we expect the kids not to reinforce one another's pathology.

When I confronted Dennis about being irresponsible, his reaction was immediate anger. "It's none of your damn business," he snapped at me. "It's my apartment and I'll do what I want there."

"Don't tell me it's not my business," I countered. "If you and Mark and the other kids are involved it certainly *is* my business. And there are things we *can* do about it. We still have custody of Mark—"

Before I could finish Dennis jumped at me. He didn't strike me, but he grabbed me and jerked me off the bed where we had been sitting, and threatened me with his upraised fist.

"Listen, you goddam bitch!" he yelled, "don't you think you can tell me what to do—"

Moe rushed into the room. Before he got through the door Dennis had already let go of me and was acting confused. I knew that very shortly that behavior would yield to the contrite and seductive game.

"Something has to be done," I told Moe, "I can't go on with this!"

In a few moments a group had formed in the living room, to talk about the problem between Dennis and me. The discussion dragged on and on because Dennis and I could not agree on the issue. He kept insisting on talking about the party, now perfectly willing to admit that he had been wrong. He apologized for his irresponsibility in exposing the younger boys to drugs. He admitted his negligence. But he kept trying to avoid talking about his relationship with me.

I was determined that, this time, we would talk about it, and get something done.

"I'm not interested in talking about the party!" I insisted. "I want to talk about the game where you get angry and hit me."

"But I didn't hit you!" Dennis protested.

"I don't care about that," I told him. "It's the same game. There's something very wrong in our relationship. I refuse to spend the rest of my life being scared by you!"

"I don't know what it's all about," Dennis cried. "I can't work it out. I would if I could, believe me!"

He looked around, pleadingly, at the circle of faces, knowing that none of them believed him. In our household people are not allowed to say, "I can't work it out."

No one came to his defense. Finally he turned back to me. There was a change in his expression. He was very serious, and when he spoke, his words were perfectly straight.

"Mom, if I try to do it, I'm really afraid that I might lose everything. I'm afraid I could end up back in the hospital."

"Do you know what it is you need to do?" I asked him. He nodded silently. "Then you have to do it," I told him.

"We'll take care of you, son," Moe told him. "You have to trust us."

Dennis looked around the circle again, his face very flushed. We all waited in silence. Finally he nodded and rose from his chair. The kids began moving the furniture, to clear the way for his acting out. The group re-formed with the boys in front, nearest Dennis, and the girls sitting in protected positions. Dennis sat down on the floor in the center of the circle. He took off his shoes and put them out of the way. I took his watch and his belt and put them safely away and then sat down on the floor facing him.

Dennis looked around at the expectant group and said in a tense, quiet voice, "I may not get through this."

"Can you tell us what you're going to do?" I asked him.

"I need to try to get through the anger to the fear. I know where the problem is in my Child, but I can't get past the anger. I know I'm going to be very young and very angry. I can feel it in my jaw and my mouth now, so I guess it's oral."

He dropped his eyes and I thought he was going to begin. Then he looked up at me again.

"If I can't get through it, will you tell me to cathect Adult?" he asked. "I will try to respond to that. I'll try to remember."

"You'll get through it, Dennis," I told him. "You've gotten through a lot of things."

"But this is the big one," he told me. "This is where it all begins."

Then, almost immediately, he began doubling up into angry contortions. Within seconds, he was a baby, red and furious, flailing and convulsing with frantic baby rage.

Along with everyone else, I jumped to hold him. His teeth clamped down on the little finger of my left hand. I could not disengage it and I realized with a shock that he was trying to bite off the finger. He only released it when his jaws were forcibly pried apart.

The struggle went on and on. After nearly two hours during which we spelled each other holding him, all of us were exhausted. But Dennis looked as though he might be able to continue indefinitely.

As Moe and I looked around at the exhausted group, we had to admit defeat.

"You'd better tell him to stop," Moe said. "We can't handle much more."

"Dennis," I leaned over him, "we can't do it. You'll have to cathect Adult."

He lay silent, motionless, on the floor. Obviously he had heard the words. But his body was still tense with anger. Watching him, I suddenly became frightened. Could Dennis have been right? Could it really be that after all we had worked through, he could still lose everything now?

I told myself that it wasn't possible. He was so far along, functional and self-sufficient in most areas. There was so much healthy structure to fall back on. He surely could not lose it all in a single episode.

After another hour had passed and Dennis had still made no intelligent response to anything we were saying to him, it did seem possible. I clung desperately to Moe, alternately angry and frightened. I had invested so much in this boy. I had tried to give him what he needed. And now it looked as though he was going to become sick again just to hurt me.

We knew that the anger Dennis was acting

out was the anger he had felt at the age of eleven months, when his mother had originally rejected him. Now he was retaliating by rejecting me and making it all my fault. I would be the cause of his getting sick again, just as his mother was responsible for his being sick in the first place.

I got up and walked out of the room, surprised at how very angry I was. It seemed incredible that after all we had accomplished together, he was doing this to me. I knew that in his mind I was being made the inadequate mother, the "not-okay" person.

When I had gone, Moe told me later, he knelt beside the immobilized boy and continued to stroke him. "You have to get out of this," he told Dennis. "You cannot give up now. She's given you up. You must call her back. You have got to make some sign."

Dennis told us later that he did it for his father.

After Moe had been talking to him and stroking him for about twenty minutes, Dennis finally gave a little mewing cry, and lifted one arm. When I was called in, he allowed me to hold him. He relaxed in my arms and the infantile cries grew into convulsive sobbing. And then, after a while, he could talk to us.

We all knew more now than we had known. Some of Dennis's infant anger had been relinquished. But we had not yet reached the fear, and we still did not know what he was afraid of.

"Anyway," Dennis concluded, "I am more in touch with the problem." He turned to me, his voice serious. "I can promise you that I will never hit you again. As for the fear—I know I have to find a way to work it out." Then, he corrected himself, "I mean *we* will have to find a way to work it out."

It was the beginning of a long, laborious process for the two of us, which we might never have concluded, had it not been for what, on the face of it, seemed our most shattering setback.

In early January I got an emergency phone call from Elizabeth's roommate. "Something's terribly wrong with Elizabeth!"

I told her to call Dennis, who was close by. A short time later Dennis called me. "It looks bad," he said. "I'm bringing her home."

They arrived a couple of hours later. I knew as soon as I looked at Elizabeth that Dennis was right. She was disheveled and distraught. Her skin was shiny and her eyes blank. When she flung herself into my lap the schizophrenia smell almost made me draw back.

We waited. Elizabeth cuddled down in my lap. "Oh, Mama," she said with a crazy little giggle. She peered around the room. "They're looking at me! Why is everyone looking at me?"

"They're concerned because you're upset," I told her.

"Upset? Mama, I feel fine!" she declared, laughing and then subsiding into giggles.

I stroked her soft hair. She made little mouth noises, and began to trace lines on my arms. At first they were light little finger strokes. Then she began to use her fingernails. "White lines," she murmured. "White. White!" The scratches got deeper and deeper.

Suddenly, with an angry cry she snatched off my wrist watch and flung it furiously across the room. "I want to kill you," she screamed. "I want to kill you! I want to kill you!"

People jumped to protect me, but Elizabeth collapsed in hysterical crying.

It was several days before we could assess what had happened.

When Elizabeth left us, she had begun, after several months, to have occasional contacts with her natural family. We knew about that, but since she had seemed to be doing so well, we had hesitated to interfere.

"You were wrong! wrong! wrong!" she told us. "Oh, if you loved me why did you let me do it?" The gist of what had happened was that she was no longer able to use the Parent part of her personality. She was all crazy Child again.

If that could happen to her, then the stability of all the youngsters who had been reparented was threatened. The other kids hastily called a meeting to discuss their own stability and to consider how they might best protect themselves from similar catastrophe. After an exhausting analysis of their personality structures and discussion of the effects of contacts with their natural families, the children arrived at the conclusion that until more was known about what had actually happened to Elizabeth none of them would risk further contact with their natural families. Some of them felt such contacts would never be safe. Others were simply unwilling to take an immediate risk.

We all worked together in a concerted effort to help Elizabeth stabilize, and to find out what had happened. Slowly, over a period of several weeks, she began to improve, although we were not sure why.

Then, just as things seemed to be settling down with her, Elizabeth fell in love.

She had first met Norman, a young Washington attorney, casually through another of our daughters and her husband. Elizabeth and Norman remet during a forty-eight-hour marathon group which another therapist and I conducted in Washington. The intense relating that is part of a marathon experience often provides an opportunity for people to get to know one another very well. I was surprised and disconcerted when Elizabeth and Norman formed a strong romantic attachment while she was still fairly upset. Moe and I didn't know what to say when, only weeks later, Norman and Elizabeth told us they wanted to get married.

If it had not been for the experience we had with Bunny and John, I think we would have reacted with an adamant, "No!" We were mainly concerned about Norman's understanding of Elizabeth's illness.

He was both responsible and informed. He understood a lot about schizophrenia and was able to clearly identify what his role, as Elizabeth's husband, should properly be in supporting and participating in her treatment. He did not appear to by playing a Rescuer game or investing in Elizabeth's pathology. "She is a very lovely young woman," he told us, "more well than sick, and I am not willing to wait for her to be completely well to be married. We'll simply deal with the problems as they come up."

Elizabeth and Norman had a beautiful wedding at the Friends Meeting House in Washington, D.C. It was not a traditional wedding—but at the last minute Elizabeth found a marvelous lace gown and gave up the bright dress she had been planning to wear. The rest of the wedding party, including the men, were dressed in vivid modern colors, and the bridal couple, as part of the ceremony, served their guests bread that I had baked for them the night before. No bride could have been happier and lovelier than Elizabeth; no parents prouder than Moe and I.

Then, the day after Elizabeth's wedding, Eric, the second of our hebephrenic children, came to live with us. As Moe and I compared his pathology with Elizabeth's, we were shocked and frightened to see how alike the two children were.

Eric and Elizabeth had met casually before, and both had reported "some kind of electricity between them." I didn't know what that was all about, but whatever the "electricity" was, I could feel it, too. The two youngsters absolutely turned each other on.

And I didn't like the way it felt.

Chapter Twelve

WHEN I BEGAN WORKING with Elizabeth I felt overwhelmed with the craziness. Against my pitiful store of information, the delusions, confusion and violence had seemed almost insurmountable problems. I approached working with Eric much more confidently, constantly asking myself how I could use what I had learned from Elizabeth and the other schizophrenic kids to penetrate the secrets of hebephrenia.

We had learned that schizophrenics are script-bound. They will become whatever they are defined to be. And during the early phase of a regression a schizophrenic youngster is fantastically vulnerable to suggestion. I immediately began telling Eric that he was able to communicate what was going on.

"You know what is happening in your head," I said many times. "You can account for everything you do or feel."

"I can?" he would echo, with Elizabeth-like naïveté.

"You certainly can!" I told him. "You are going to have to give me a lot of information so I can know how to help you."

As we began to acquire an understanding of hebephrenia, Elizabeth caught on to the idea of using theory to understand and solve the problems still confronting her. The two youngsters began sharing information about their backgrounds, feelings, and perceptions. Almost as alike in their experience as identical twins who had grown up in the same household, they infected one another with an electric kind of excitement as they achieved one milestone after another in explaining what had happened to them.

And we watched them, comparing, learning, and after a short time believing that in the secrets behind the hebephrenic pathology lay all the clues to schizophrenia.

The hebephrenic child is afraid of starvation. Both Elizabeth and Eric's natural mothers reported an unsuccessful attempt in nursing the children. The urge to suck is one of the earliest survival behaviors observable in an infant; this need was still present in both of the kids when they first came to us. However, although they could identify the need, they were unable to suck energetically at the bottles we offered them. And this seemed to be a result of their mothers' reactions to nursing them.

When they regressed to a period immediately following their births, Elizabeth and Eric both reported feeling desperately hungry, but not daring to suck vigorously—believing that if they attempted to gratify the urge the flow of milk would cease or their mothers would remove the breast. Their only hope of being fed at all was to lap passively at the nipple.

When I gave Eric a bottle he would put his

hands between his legs, clasping them tightly with his knees. He believes his mother put his hands in that position so that he could not touch her breast. Both youngsters are convinced that their mothers were sexually stimulated by their nursing and that their later problems with sex, as well as the whole pathological pattern, was predicated on this problem.

Their mothers reported that Elizabeth and Eric were unusually good babies. What the children say is that they learned not to cry when they needed attention, because they would then be ignored until they stopped crying. The only way they could hope to receive care was to wait passively until their mothers decided to come to them.

It hurts to be hungry. Most babies cry when they are hungry. But these babies learned that a crying, fussy baby might not get fed at all. So they had to pretend that the hunger did not exist. They learned to separate their hunger and the anger that went with the fear of starvation from the sweet-and-good adaptive behavior which provided the only key to maternal care. If they were good babies, their mothers might pay attention to them. If they were bad, angry or crying, they were deserted.

Ultimately, a kind of classical Jekyll-Hyde personality structure emerged. The behaviors the babies demonstrated to their mothers were a kind of happy, cooperative passivity. But a second personality, frantically hungry and homicidally angry also developed.

As a child grows, learns to play and crawl and

walk, he learns new ways to make demands on his mother's attention. Elizabeth and Eric report that they never had this kind of experience. As they grew more active, a new way of reinforcing the fear of starvation was begun. Elizabeth remembers being tied in a bed, "so she wouldn't throw off her covers." Elizabeth says the confinement, in a kind of harness attached to the mattress of her crib, was used to get her out of the way if she fussed or was otherwise demanding.

Eric was kept in a playpen until his third year, "because he was sickly and might catch cold." When he tried to climb out of the playpen it was put on stilts so he could not escape. Eric remembers looking at the world through bars. He remembers how much he wanted to get out. He was teased by an older sister and unable to defend himself. He dared not display any anger because if he did his mother would simply walk out of the room, leaving him penned, helpless, and alone.

And always the hunger. Babies believe their mothers know how they feel; it never occurred to Elizabeth or Eric that their mothers did not know they were hungry. The crying with which most babies signal their needs had long since been extinguished as a means of communication, and the passivity, sitting quietly and smiling sweetly, was the only way these babies knew to signal the need for care.

At about two years of age children experience a stage of negativism which is an important part of healthy development. For no good reason, the child begins to feel angry much of the time, and he begins to misbehave for no apparent purpose other than to annoy his mother and find out what he can get away with. The mother and child are locked in conflict, and the result is that the child learns that he is separate from his mother. Resulting from this discovery, the Adult part of his personality, memory, problem-solving, and more mature thinking, emerges, and is the means by which the child learns to get what he wants and needs and still conform to the expectations of the world around him.

That didn't happen with Elizabeth and Eric. Convinced that any expression of anger would have terrible consequences, they internalized the negativism, adding the anger to the store of feelings already separated from the smiling faces and seductive manner they presented to the world.

Another problem was that neither child could develop a value system or understand the values of people around them. Morals are incorporated as a means of controlling unacceptable behavior. Elizabeth and Eric originally learned to adapt to their mothers, but as they grew older they adapted to the immediate situation in which they found themselves. The means by which they accomplished such complete conformity was to deny any feelings or ideas which were inconsistent with the immediate situations. Thus, values could not be carried over from one situation and applied in another situation. Both youngsters could naïvely engage in bizarre, dangerous, or immoral behavior without a second thought if it were suggested or supported by the group they were with at the time. Later, when confronted with someone who thought what they had done was wrong, the conflict of values left them confused and passive. "I'll be a stone," Elizabeth would say. Eric would simply stand and look blankly miserable until someone rescued him.

Adolescence is a time of resolution. Because the child is older, can think better, and has more resources in the world around him, problems which have not been resolved in earlier years come up again and are often settled. Those problems which can't be worked out result in pathology. Both Elizabeth and Eric tried desperately to find a way through the turmoil of adolescence. The oral needs crowded in on them and no adequate mothering was available. They tried to find a solution to the lack of a value system in religion and were unsuccessful. When Elizabeth entered the convent she was trying to find safety in the structured religious life. Eric was sent to a military school at age thirteen, and although miserably unhappy there, was able to get along because of the external controls.

There were, for both youngsters, more and more frequent outbursts of the "bad" Child; as they grew more confused and unhappy the pent-up feelings could no longer be denied. After the angry outbursts there were no clear memories of what had happened, because the denial mechanisms kept their Adults unaware. The Jekyll-Hyde pattern became more and more pronounced.

We spent a lot of time trying to find out what the children's natural parents, who seem innocent and well-meaning, did wrong, why their children grew sick, while other children who are more actively mistreated and have fewer advantages, can grow to healthy maturity.

We learned about discounting, what happens when a child's feelings or needs are discounted by the parents.

Both of these families, and the families of other hebephrenic children we have known, practice a great deal of denial. When they don't know how to solve a problem, they find a way to discount it, to pretend it doesn't exist. Although Eric was seriously undernourished all through his childhood, he was never told that he should eat, and the consequences of his not eating were never explained. When, in a fit of rage he kicked a hole in the bathroom wall, his parents, without asking him what had happened, decided that it was an accident. When Elizabeth's parents found out that she was stealing clothing from department stores, they did not bring it up to her. "We thought it was a stage she would outgrow."

There are various ways to discount. If a child is crying, the mother can go to sleep or turn on the radio or otherwise avoid hearing the crying, thus discounting that there is a problem. Or she can discount her ability to do anything about the problem, "I just don't know what is the matter with him." Or she can discount that there is a reason for the crying, "Some babies just cry a lot." Or she can discount that there is a solution to the problem, "Nothing will satisfy him."

One of the reasons our children get well, the major reason Elizabeth did so well with us when we didn't understand what was happening, was that we try not to discount. We consider all behavior purposeful and try always to confront it in some way. However, before we knew what had happened to hebephrenic children, and realized the role discounting always plays in the development of schizophrenia, we had no concept of how important that policy was to the children's getting well.

Both Elizabeth and Eric were scripted to discount by their parents. Eric's parents did not see that he got enough to eat or teach him about nutrition, and when nutrition was studied in school, Eric simply didn't pay attention or read the book, getting an F on his report card. Both children discounted pain, since experiencing pain would include feeling hungry. Neither could tell the difference between hot and cold because they were not supposed to feel. Being spanked for misbehavior was an important experience for these children, partly because it was a way of demanding that they be responsible for behavior, but even more because spanking is based on the expectation that the child will feel pain, and was a major means by which the kids got permission to experience feelings. (Neither had ever been spanked by their natural parents.)

One of the most dramatic discoveries occurred by accident. Elizabeth was visiting and we were trying to work out some of the pathology the youngsters shared, when Eric got into a quarrel with a group of kids. The kids were angry with his discounting, and when they described what had happened, I recognized the behavior as something I had seen Eric do on other occasions. "All right, so let's forget it," he would say angrily, or, "You can't prove that!" It was unusual behavior for Eric, and on the occasions it had happened it had made me furious.

I had thought that Eric's discounting came from his Child and was an adaptation to his natural parents, but as I listened, I suddenly realized that was wrong. He was telling other people what they should do. That behavior was from the Parent Ego State!

I was momentarily puzzled. Eric had gotten rid of his Parent Ego State several weeks before and I had not seen an instance where the decathected Parent had recurred. Moreover, what I had seen of Eric's Parent was quite different from this behavior.

Excitedly I grabbed a piece of paper and drew a picture, the circles TA therapists use to describe ego states. But instead of one Parent, I drew two, one for the Sweet and Good part of the Child and one for the Bad, denied Child. What had happened, I realized, was that the children had perceived their natural parents as divided in the same way they were. The Jekyll and the Hyde parts of their personalities had each known a completely different kind of parenting. The Sweet and Good Child had incorporated a silly, insipid Parent that didn't control behavior or nurture effectively. The Bad Child incorporated an angry, evil Parent that discounted and was homicidal. "If you are bad, I'll let you starve."

I saw Elizabeth and Eric go white as the whole denial mechanism began to crumble.

Then they began to get high. As we got them into the living room, began telephoning for help and preparing for the episodes we knew were imminent, they got higher and higher, in a frantic attempt to hold everything together.

"Frog!" Eric said.

"Plog!" Elizabeth replied.

They both jiggled and giggled, boys on either side trying to hold them down. They made strange mouth noises which sent them into peals of hysterical laughter. Seemingly they understood one another perfectly. "Gluck!" said Elizabeth.

"Cluck!" Eric responded.

"Wuck! Muck! Fuck!" Elizabeth crowed triumphantly.

Both children were convinced they were going to die, and in the midst of the giddiness there were moments of rationality. "Oh Mama," Elizabeth cried, "I'm going to burn up! I'm going to explode!"

"I'm going to burn up and be a vegetable!" Eric prophesied, his voice frantic. "All the energy will burn me up!"

"That can't happen, can it Mom?" one of the children asked. "They're going to be okay?"

I looked around at the roomful of children and remembered that I had promised never to lie to them. I knew they were all awaiting my answer. And I thought of the hebephrenics I had seen in the hospitals. "Burned out," is how they are often described. The frenetic energy is spent and they feel and look like empty shells. Vegetables. I wondered how Eric, who had never seen such patients, knew about that. Unless he had simply guessed from what was happening inside him.

I tried to answer calmly. "I don't know exactly what's happening," I said. "I can't promise anything. But I think Elizabeth and Eric know what they need to do and they have to find a way to do it."

Before the children let go, Moe and other help arrived, and it was fortunate that we had enough people, because it took ten strong men to hold Elizabeth and twelve to hold Eric.

We had seen primitive anger before, but I had never imagined anything like this. They writhed and convulsed, their faces furious masks, obviously out of touch with what was going on around them. They bit and fought the people holding them; the rug under them was drenched with sweat. Elizabeth fought for a half hour; Eric went on for nearly an hour.

And then it was over. Both children were limp, bruised and exhausted, but both were rational.

We were not able to talk to the children that evening, so I eagerly awakened Eric the next morning. For the first time, I noticed, there was no fresh blood on his mouth and pillow, although his mouth was chewed from the evening before. "How do you feel?" I asked eagerly.

He looked at me, little-boy sleepy. "I've got a new Child," he told me. "I never felt like this before."

"How is it different?"

He raised up on his elbow, grimacing from the sore muscles. "I don't think I'm crazy any more," he said. "I can't exactly explain that. I don't think I could have a hallucination or anything like that."

What we had just seen we would soon begin to call "the hebephrenic resolution." It took us several days to assess the changes and to arrange psychological testing. Elizabeth had not been actively psychotic at the time, so the changes were difficult to assess in her. She also, as Eric did, maintained that she had a "new Child." Obviously the Good Child/Bad Child dichotomy was gone; both children were confused and distressed when they discovered that they were having "good" and "bad" impulses at the same time. "How do people decide what to do?" Elizabeth wailed at one point. "How can I sort it out?" The improvement in Eric was very apparent. The delusional thinking seemed completely gone, the psychosis resolved. With both youngsters the giddiness and silliness, the naïveté and suggestibility subsided.

The dichotomy was broken down. The discounting Parent Ego State was also gone. "There isn't anything inside my head that wants to kill me now," Eric reported. "Now we can really get well," Elizabeth added.

But things did not go so smoothly. Over the next several months we tried to help both youngsters get used to having "good" and "bad" feelings combined, and only became more convinced that a healthy maturity can't be based on an abnormal childhood. For Elizabeth and Norman the problem became more urgent when they learned that Elizabeth was pregnant.

After several months of struggling, Eric regressed and a few weeks later Elizabeth, too, came home to be a baby again. At the same time Shirley decided to come home and be born for the last time. The new integrated Child in each of them could now experience a healthy infancy.

From the hebephrenic babies and Shirley we learned how real a regression has to be, that a baby must be a baby, can't be expected to think like a university student, and should not have to use his Adult.

Now we put all our babies in diapers and feed them from bottles and let them sleep as much as they like. When they are hungry they cry; both Elizabeth and Eric had trouble learning to do that. When they are older they chew on teething rings and pretzels and start eating traditional baby foods. Eventually they learn to crawl, to talk, and begin to feed themselves. The two-year-old negativistic stage is always a problem; for a while I thought Eric might never get toilet trained.

If we meet the child's needs during the regression, the need for therapy is almost completely eliminated. At every developmental stage we are confronted with a disturbed child and the disturbance must be successfully resolved so the child can have the experience of functioning like a normal, healthy little boy or girl. It really isn't so difficult to resolve those problems, because every child has within him a tremendous drive to grow up healthy and happy, and only needs parents who will love him and respond to his needs.

Before we understood hebephrenia our kids were getting well, not because we understood what we were doing, but because of our own natural responses to them and their needs. Perhaps we hadn't understood what to do for Elizabeth, for Dennis, and the other early kids, because we weren't yet ready to depart so radically from traditional treatment.

But in the three years since Dennis had come to us, Moe and I had grown a lot too.

Chapter Thirteen

DENNIS HAD AN EXCELLENT year at the University. His grades were all A's and B's and we liked the new circle of friends he was developing in Charlottesville. He came home nearly every weekend, and continued to be actively involved with the family. By now there was no obvious pathology and Moe and I were convinced that whatever the problems in our relationships, Dennis was as completely our son as any child could be.

We made him ours legally before he graduated from college, renaming him Aaron Wolfe Schiff—Aaron, a solid Hebrew name we all liked—Wolfe for an old friend of mine.

Aaron was now as invested as we were in working out the problems in his relationship to me, and we continued a long, slow, sometimes disheartening process of identifying and working through each specific step of the problem.

The first major hurdle was his belief that I wanted to castrate him. Aaron was not afraid of castration. He seemed to regard the idea with a kind of morbid pleasure.

"It sounds as though you want to be castrated." I exclaimed in exasperation.

"Maybe I do," he answered seriously. "At

least the part of me that believes you want to castrate me is willing to go along with that."

"Has it occurred to you that it would be pretty painful?" I asked.

"I doubt it," he shrugged indifferently. "It wouldn't hurt very much."

We spent a lot of fruitless and frustrating time talking about why he thought I wanted to castrate him. I finally gave up on that, and began to concentrate, instead, on his lack of investment in his own masculinity.

The problem continued to be unresolved. Aaron had to decide for himself that he was unwilling to sacrifice his manhood for mothering, and I finally decided to take a chance on a confrontation which was both bizarre and extreme.

Naked, Aaron was strapped securely in a restraining chair. As I approached him with a large hunting knife, I was sure that he believed I would, indeed, castrate him. To my dismay, he did not appear in the least frightened.

Maybe he really did want to be castrated! I thought fleetingly of those men who have submitted to surgery in order to become as much like females as they could be made. I remembered how desperately Aaron had wanted the love he saw his mother lavish on her daughters. Perhaps mutilation was worth it, in his thinking, to get that love.

Then, as I laid the edge of the knife against his naked genitals, Aaron's face drained of color.

"What am I going to do?" I asked him. "Shall I start cutting so you can never be a man?"

"No, no please!" he whispered. "I want to be a man. Mom, I *do* want to be a man!"

"I don't believe you," I said. I pressed slightly with the knife, and his controls broke. He began to struggle and scream.

Untied and safe, the knife put away, Aaron lay shaking in my arms as I stroked and reassured him. "I want you to be a man," I told him. "I love you as much as I could love a daughter."

Again, through Aaron we had learned something new; the chance I took had paid off. The castration problem in paranoia cannot be resolved by reassuring the child he will not be castrated. It *can* be overcome by resolving the impulses in the child that would allow such a thing to happen. By being forced to confront and take responsibility for his own wish for self-mutilation the paranoid can successfully be made to affirm his right to his sexuality. But this can only be accomplished when treatment is far enough along, as it was with Aaron, that the child has a real investment in his own worth.

Later, when Mark erupted into pathological outbursts around his castration fears, Aaron took on the problem with his brother. "Look," he challenged, "the next time you feel castrated, just let me know. What I'll do is, I'll kick you right in the balls. Then you'll know you've still got them." Mark stared at Aaron with shocked expression. That was enough to stop his paranoid episodes altogether.

After the resolution of the castration problem we bogged down. On the surface Aaron was affectionate and polite, but underlying the relationship with me was a passive-aggressive game that seemed unresolvable.

The pattern was always the same. Things would be going smoothly between us, and then Aaron would misperceive something that happened. He would angrily accuse me of something I had not done. When confronted with reality, he would either become seductively contrite, or, as time went on and he understood that would not work, he would discount my feelings altogether.

An example was an incident around a car. I had asked Aaron to take care of delivering the car to someone and he promised that he would. Later, when the people telephoned to find out what had happened, Aaron denied any memory of it. "You're always doing that!" he yelled. "You think you've told me something when you haven't and then try to blame it on me!" Confronted by people who were present and remembered the incident, Aaron admitted he was wrong, but continued to be furious. "It's exactly the kind of thing you would do," he insisted.

Sometimes I challenged his outbursts of irrational anger. At other times it seemed pointless to get into a quarrel which I knew by now would end in frustration, and I didn't bother to confront him.

When we discussed the game, Aaron insisted that I was the cause of it. "There is something you should do that you aren't doing," he kept telling us. "I could work it out if you would just do what you should."

Sometimes he turned angrily on Moe. "No

matter what she says or does, you support her," he accused. "You never even stop to think if it's right!"

"Aaron, you can't be right when you make up things to be mad about," Moe responded, exasperated. "I support her because I think she's right."

We had learned a lot from the hebephrenic babies, and the key to the game with Aaron eventually came from our experiences with them.

Elizabeth and Eric never learned to identify and think about those feelings which their mothers discounted. They were both masters of passivity, and from them I began to understand that passive-aggressive behavior must come from the oral stage of development, that when a child is confused about separating what he is doing from what someone else is doing there has probably been a serious disruption in his outgrowing the symbiotic relationship with his mother which was natural as an infant.

I realized that Aaron felt something he could not define because, bright and aware as he was, he had not been taught to define it.

Finally I stumbled onto a clue that supported Aaron's complaints. We were rehashing a quarrel from some months earlier, and Aaron said, "I wish you hadn't walked out! Why do you always walk out in situations like that?"

I thought about the incident. Aaron had been acting unreasonably hostile and rude, and I had simply left the room. "What else can I do?" I asked him. "When you act like that there doesn't seem to be any way I can stop you."

"Why didn't you hit me?" he asked earnestly. "Why didn't you do *something*?" I was astonished to see tears in his eyes.

After puzzling about it and discussing it with Moe, I still felt unsettled, and finally I brought it up with Rich Epstein, a young psychiatrist who does consultations for us.

"You know," Rich mused "there might be something there. Has it ever occurred to you that you might overreact to passive-aggressive behavior?"

I stared at him in astonishment. Had I in fact been contributing to the passive-aggressive exchange by expressing my own anger in an unstraight way—by doing nothing? When a person forgets or discounts what others expect of him, it is often an angry behavior.

My typical reaction to passive-aggressive behavior was to walk out on it. Instead of getting angry, I would shrug if off. "That's your problem," I would say, when Aaron discounted my feelings. "Don't expect me to get excited about it."

With Rich I began to realize that my reaction to passive-aggressive behavior was passive-aggressive! By refusing to deal with Aaron's behavior, I was duplicating and reinforcing that behavior.

When I felt convinced that I understood what was happening, I discussed with Aaron what I was finding out about myself.

His voice was husky when he responded. "I'm

just beginning to realize how much you care about me," he said.

The way to stop a game is to confront the discounting behavior by using your Adult. Instead, my scared Child was simply copping out and retreating from the situations. As soon as I stopped doing that, my relationship with Aaron improved; so did my relationship with Rickey and the other latency-age boys (about eight to twelve years) in the family.

Now when Aaron was passive-aggressive I consistently confronted him, and we began to find out what his anger was all about. At first he reacted with surprise, often with anger. But when he discovered that his anger no longer frightened me, he seemed to be relieved, and became more cooperative.

Within a short time we were able to come up with the script from Aaron's natural family which had programmed his becoming sick and crazy. I was not surprised that it came from his mother rather than from his paranoid father, nor was it unexpected that it arose from passive-aggressive behavior on her part.

The clue to the script is apparent in the fantasy which first triggered Aaron's regression—when he was flogging his father while his mother stood by passively. We began to understand that her passivity meant to Aaron that she wanted him to do crazy, violent things.

Aaron was able to recall how his mother stood passively by and let his father do crazy things. She never seemed embarrassed or tried to interfere. He believed that she took secret enjoyment in the crazy acts, that she got gratification from this evidence that men are "not-all-right."

As Aaron grew older, he was aware that his mother never taught him to behave appropriately, as other children's mothers taught them. She never disciplined him, let him go to school looking strange as compared to the other children, was disinterested in any constructive interests he developed. This also confirmed his belief that she wanted him to be different.

When Aaron talked to his mother about his impulses to kill his father, whom he believed she hated, as he believed she hated all men, she did not say, "Its wrong to kill people," or even, "Don't do it." What she told him was, "If you can hold out until you go to college then you can get out of it."

Aaron believed his mother wanted him to kill his father, and that was the only way he could win her love. But she offered him an alternative. That was to leave home and never come back. Torn between the father who had loved him and cared for him, desperate for the mothering he was denied, the problem seemed unsolvable. He left home at seventeen, knowing he would not go back. He had a script to be crazy with no alternatives. If he tried to return home, he must kill his father. He had nowhere to go and no one to trust.

When my "walking out" seemed to duplicate what his natural mother had done, Aaron perceived the same sick messages, and felt confronted by the same unresolvable conflict: "Act crazy." "Kill your father." "Men are not okay."

"You can never get my love." It was only when I began confronting the game that Aaron began to believe I didn't want him to be angry or crazy. All our quarrels had arisen from his thinking I wanted him to be irrationally angry.

It also became apparent that Aaron was jealous of my relationship with some of the other children, especially Chucky, with whom he believed I had a freer, more spontaneous Child-to-Child relationship.

"You never liked my Child," Aaron accused me. "You only relate to my Adult."

From Aaron's point of view that seemed a fair charge. I enjoy children who are spontaneous and expressive. When Aaron first regressed Moe and I were unsure about how much of his regression we should support and we had consistently supported his using his Adult. He had often been difficult and demanding, and I realized that I had been most affectionate toward him at times when he was being passive. His whining and seductiveness and temper tantrums had never been resolved because we had avoided confronting them, and the natural spontaneity of his Child was still dammed up behind his adaptive behavior.

And now, again because of the hebephrenic babies, we know what to do. Aaron's Child still needed to experience the unconditional love which neither his natural mother nor I had ever offered him.

We made baby gowns for Aaron from old monk's robes donated to us by our Trappist friends at the Holy Cross Abbey in Berryville,

and made huge diapers by sewing together six
diapers.

Aaron came home and settled into his third,
and final infancy. This time there were no games
between us, and the anger dissipated. I was his
mother and if he was hungry or wet or upset, he
had to let me take care of him. He learned that I
would and could take care of him, that he did
not have to use his intelligence to be loved, that
it was all right to be a boy child. In only a few
weeks he was able to give up the seductiveness
and tantrums and become a spontaneous, responsive little boy, and then a happy, productive
man.

The most important thing Aaron learned was
that he was okay and I was okay.

Chapter Fourteen

As BUNNY GOT WELL, gaining in both physical strength and emotional stability, she and John both talked about becoming therapists. Bunny's interest in working with children was partly due to her identification with me. The fact that she could not have children of her own was also a motivating factor. Schizophrenics often have difficulty getting pregnant, and for a while we had all hoped that her trouble originated in the emotional, rather than physical problem. When this did not prove true, Bunny was sadly disappointed.

"But your drawing seems so really important," I told her. "I'm not comfortable with your developing a vocational interest in something so different."

"I want to work with children," Bunny insisted. "And so does John. If we worked together, I could still draw."

During the two years that Bunny was with us, John had become an active and involved member of the family. He was by now familiar with all the problems of the household, and was a regular, and experienced, participant in family groups. Moe and I both believed that the kind of reparenting we were doing could be carried on by other couples who were equally committed. Our friends, the Faulkers, with our encouragement, had already successfully reparented one schizophrenic child in their home, and had taken another.

Gradually the idea of opening a second house in Fredericksburg, in which Bunny and John would be the parents took shape.

The Christy house opened in May 1969 with five children. These children are all wards of the Project. At present our own household consists of Moe and me, our natural children and twenty children who are either in our personal custody or are wards of the Project. We have recently added a trainee program which brings enthusiastic young therapists into our community for work and training each year. Their presence adds immeasurably to our ability to consolidate what we have learned and contribute to the pool of knowledge and techniques applied to the care and treatment of many children across the country whom we cannot personally reach.

Since our enlarged Project required additional space for office and staff housing, we recently acquired a building on the edge of town, which provides offices for Moe and me, staff living quarters, and a separate lower level, opening onto a large parking lot, which has become Eric's Natural Child Coffee House.

Here, Eric and several other musicians in our family, including Mark and Bob, and guest entertainers drawn from the area perform three nights per week. There is space for fifty, and the Natural Child is usually crowded to capacity.

When the coffee house first opened, Moe and I were worried about its effect on our public relations but the experience of mixing our kids and their music with the community has proved rewarding for all.

More and more Moe and I think of what we are doing as a life style rather than a method of treatment. Using Transactional Analysis first as a treatment technique, and later as a starting point for initiating our own research, we now seem to have developed a style of relating that is infectious. "It's a powerful thing," our friends tell us. "You walk in the door—any door—your house, the Christys' house, the coffee shop—and it hits you. It's not just that people are getting well. It means more than that."

I want much more for all my children than mental health. I want them to have the opportunity to experience life fully. I want them to have the stability and security that enables them to be spontaneous and creative. I want them to be expressive with one another and involved with the world around them. Perhaps more than anything else, I want them to go out into the world knowing how to love and be loved.

There were nearly fifty of us together at Passover for the Seder, smaller than last year's one hundred, since we decided not to invite anyone but family and a few very special guests. Families develop traditions, and the Seder is one of our most meaningful ones.

Most of the seventeen children who have been successfully reparented were at home. I missed those who weren't there. John B. was sick. One of the Trues' twins had mumps, so none of their family could come. Gracie is being anti-tradition. Children grow up, and of course they don't always come home, even for special occasions.

We had to prepare a cold dinner because the ritual takes a long time, and our ovens, in anticipation of the holiday, were out of order. But there was lamb and chicken and ginger meat balls, and all of the things the kids expect for a Seder. Getting ready wasn't too much of a hassle because I'm finally learning how to prepare for holidays and defend myself against the inevitable commotion and endless demands of excited children. I've learned to delegate instead of being personally responsible for every clean skirt and pair of shined shoes.

Probably the Seder is most important to Moe. He enjoys the role of Jewish patriarch. He likes to look proudly over the sons and daughters gathered around him. "Be fruitful and multiply...."

There are grandchildren too. Ian, Eric's little boy, has been living with us for several months. He is a vivacious little two-year-old, and impatient with tedious ritual when he is hungry. Elizabeth and Norman arrived with their newborn twins, who cried during the Seder service, but slept nicely through dinner. Chucky is in love, for the first time I guess, and the girl was with him. He stayed very near her, touching, protecting, proud and somehow very vulnerable.

Frank Andruzzi, who works for us, and his wife Janet, who are very much part of the family have their little girl, two months old now, and huge beside Elizabeth's six-pound twins.

The Christys brought the newest regressed baby from their house. And our two newest babies, Johnny and Eddy, sit on the floor near the front. Both are remarkably good during the service, but anxious to get to the food part.

Moe asks different boys to read part of the service. Rickey begins, standing very straight but obviously glad when it's over. Aaron gets through his part without lisping. I hadn't realized before what a powerful reading voice Bob had, although it's certainly loud and clear when he parents younger children. John S. didn't seem as scared as usual when reading aloud.

I think briefly of Rosita, of the other children who did not get well, wishing they were here, that things could be different. Then I make myself stop thinking about that.

I look around at the children, and I am so proud of them. I know that they are beautiful and that we have helped to bring out the beauty. I know, too, that they give us back as much as we can ever give to them. Raising children, watching them grow, helping them get well, is a good thing for us to be doing. I can feel the warmth, the intimacy in the room, throughout the whole house, the "special feeling" visitors tell us about.

Moe asks Eric to play *Fall Rain*, the song he wrote for the family, and dedicated to us:

Fall may bring the rain, my love
Fall may bring the rain
If both of us were child again
The dreams might be the same
They'd be the same
Might be the same . . .

I could not buy you happiness
I cannot grant you peace
But I can hold you softly, love
And stroke away your grief
Stroke away your grief. . . .

The children's voices pick up the refrain, singing softly, full of the meaning of the words.

I feel Moe's hand tighten on my shoulder and I glance around to see tears in his eyes.

"When I hear that," he says quietly, "then I know it's all been worthwhile."

I nod, and give his hand a squeeze, agreeing with him.

There is still so much to learn, so many unanswered questions. But we know now that answers can be found.

Our kids are getting well.

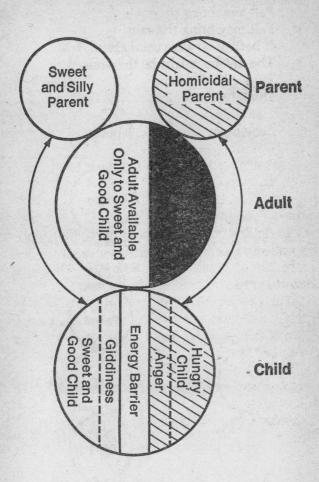

EGO STATES IN HEBEPHRENIA

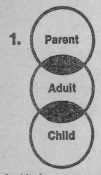

1.

Just before a regression
the Parent and Child
are in conflict
and drain energy
from the Adult.

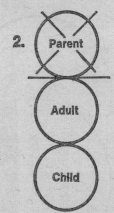

2.

The conflict is resolved by
excluding and decathecting
the crazy Parent.

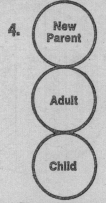

3.

The new Parent is
incorporated.

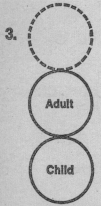

4.

The new Parent is
cathected.

REPARENTING

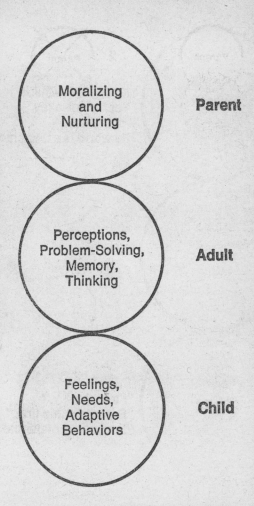

EGO STATES

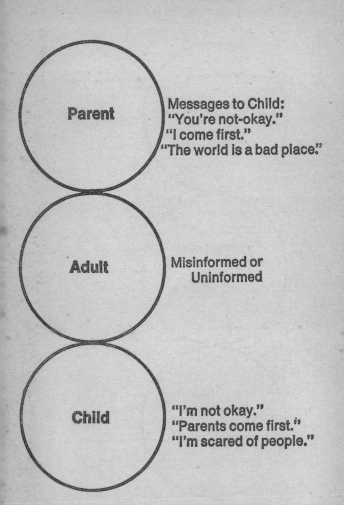

Parent — Messages to Child:
"You're not-okay."
"I come first."
"The world is a bad place."

Adult — Misinformed or Uninformed

Child — "I'm not okay."
"Parents come first."
"I'm scared of people."

EGO STATES IN SCHIZOPHRENIA